In Love Under New Management

Other Books by the Gwendolyn Ann Cook

"The Power to Believe"
It's not what you need, it's what you Believe!

"The Intercessor, God's Secretary"
Reminding God of His Word

In Love Under New Management

A LOVE THAT'S ETERNAL

BY

GWENDOLYN ANN COOK

authorHOUSE®

AuthorHouse™
1663 Liberty Drive
Bloomington, IN 47403
www.authorhouse.com
Phone: 1 (800) 839-8640

Published by AuthorHouse 11/18/2015

ISBN: 978-1-5049-5639-0 (sc)
ISBN: 978-1-5049-5638-3 (e)

Print information available on the last page.

Any people depicted in stock imagery provided by Thinkstock are models, and such images are being used for illustrative purposes only. Certain stock imagery © *Thinkstock.*

This book is printed on acid-free paper.

© 1997 Merriam-Webster, Incorporated,
Springfield Massachusetts. U.S.A.
© 1999 Langenscheidt Publishers, Inc. New York

TABLE OF CONTENTS

SPECIAL THANKS TO:

Rev. Dr. Eve Lynne Rowena Fenton, Founder & President of *"Women In Covenant,"* as well as my mentor. Thanks for your God given gifts, which enables you to speak into the lives of thousands of women, as well as your heart felt assistance in mentoring me into my divine purpose. Your guidance and support have truly inspired me while on this journey of being a woman of God, as well as a woman of purpose. Thank you for unselfishly giving of your time!

Mayor Carolyn V. Chang, Mayor of *"Westampton, New Jersey"* and the *Carolyn V. Chang, Law Office.* Your friendship brings with it an abundance of wisdom and guidance helping to keep me moving forward at all cost. You have the ability to speak truth to power as you pave the way for women all over the world; you are surely making a difference in the lives of so many young women of color. I knew when we first met it was going to be a divine connection, thanks for assisting me in living out my purpose.

Dr. Jannah Scott, Th.D., Deputy Director
DHS Center for Faith-based & Neighborhood Partnerships

A Center of the White House Office of Faith-based and Neighborhood Partnerships. Dr. Jannah I especially thank you for your leadership skills, and the unwavering friendship that we have, as well as your willingness to consider me to be one of your colleagues in the work that God has called you to. Your ability to assist in bringing recovery to cities with the understanding that this will only be successful when together we enlist the agency of prayer. A gigantic thanks for taking me along for the journey; you are truly a woman of God, grace and purpose.

To my special friend Dana Redd the Mayor of the City that both you and I so truly love. I thank God for bringing us together in such a divine way. I recall our first meeting when I had the opportunity to interview you on TBN, your heart felt expression for the love of God as well as the love you have for Camden and its residence were evident. Thanks for seeing the gifts that God has so generously distributed in me for the work of moving our youth forward in the City of Camden. Thanks for your ongoing support and belief in me!

DEDICATIONS

To my late father SGM George Albert Greene (daddy), whose love and parenting skills has helped me to become the woman of God that I am today. Dad your guidance and unconditional love has provoked me to see that I have no limits to what I desire to do and to be. You are surly a soldier in the army of the Lord. Thanks for teaching me to march for the cause and expect the victory no matter what it looked like. You are truly my hero.

To my late mother Trillis Irene Greene (mom), you are still teaching me how to prepare for greatness. You may be absence in body but your loving spirit continues to live on teaching me to stand in the midst of all the world has to offer. Whether I encounter good or bad times, the remembrance of your encouraging words continue to help me endure and not give up. I dedicate this book to you for in the seasons when sickness and disease had me bound God used you to encourage me through those dark and stormy nights. I see so much of you in me and I commit to making you proud of whom I'm still becoming. I now, more than ever understand the gift of mothering that you possessed. Thanks for being the best mother and friend that a girl could ever have; you have truly blessed my life. Love you mom!

To my great great-niece Londyn Irene Greene, I'm so thankful that you have entered into the Kingdom of God right here in the earth; I speak a prophetic anointing over your life, that you will do great exploits for His Kingdom. My prayer for you is that even at two years old you will experience the presence of God and learn to trust Him as I do. Your ministry is already established in Him.

To the women in my immediate family, thanks for allowing God to use you as you assist me in living a life with no limits. Your ongoing encouragement and support means the world to me. Niecy you continue to love me with no conditions, Tina you inspire me to be the best that I can be by believing that I can do anything that I set my hands to. And my dear sister-in-law Angie, your sweet spirit and your push for excellence out of me has been God sent. Thank you all for being an extension of God's hand. And I definitely can't forget about my oldest sister Joy who has gone on to be with the Lord, I know that you are pulling strings in heaven on my behalf. To my oldest and only brother Robert "Bo" Greene who has always, even as a young boy been the gatekeeper over his four (4) sisters. I love you all, with every beat of my heart.

To all of the female teenagers that I have had the opportunity to tough in and through our Youth-At-Risk Mentoring Program, you have truly assisted God in helping me to build Godly character. Loving and trusting me unconditionally has inspired me to strive to be the best mentor that I can be, to help you live life not being ashamed of the gospel of Jesus Christ has been a challenge, but yet rewarding. I purpose to be there for all your successes as well as failures you may encounter. Keep looking forward and see the salvation of the Lord!

To my Lord, my Master and my Savior, You God are my all and all. You are my Great Healer, Deliverer and Friend. I thank You Father God for staying true to Your Word and leading me on this journey with the assurance that You will never leave me nor will You forsake me. Thanks for opening doors of success and closing all doors of sickness, disease and failure. You alone deserve all the glory and the honor, I sing praises to Your Name my heart truly belongs to You. I look forward to our continued journey as I on purpose move out of the way, so that You may have Your way in and through my life. Love You to the upmost!

Foreword by: Pastor Jonathan W. Cook

In Love Under New Management is an amazing account of God's ability to transform one's life from a worm like existence to a beautiful butterfly.

With a no holds bar approach Gwen is surprisingly and extremely transparent as she reveals what life was like before and after she was compelled to accept the Lord Jesus Christ as her personal Savior.

From the valley to the mountain top Gwendolyn Ann Cook does a masterful critique of her life before and after Christ, without hesitation she talks openly about life when she was at her lowest point. Driven by feeling self-hate and ambivalence, she set out on a path of promiscuous and deviant behavior.

Like so many of us Gwen was led to blindly dance with the devil, which ultimately had a profound effect on her and the lives of those she touched. However, like the Apostle Paul she learned first-hand about the significance and importance of God's grace and mercy. I was personally inspired and at times somewhat startled as she continued to be brutally honest.

I trust that you too will be inspired, encouraged and prayerfully transformed as you read this life changing account of how God personally met her while on her road to Damascus and translated her into His marvelous light.

In 1 Peter 4:8, Peter declares "for love shall cover a multitude of sins;" in and through this love, which has been authored and orchestrated by God, Gwen is able to convey how awesome falling *"In Love Under New Management,"* is.

When I consider the life style she lived and her near death experience, I am in awe of God's goodness and convinced of His love for us all. Surely like many of us her life was not meant to be lived alone but to the contrary shared with us all as a living epistle.

I strongly encourage you to sit back and allow God to personally chauffer you through her life changing experiences, which I believe is a divine call to fall *"In Love Under New Management."*

Jonathan W. Cook, Sr. Pastor
Instruments Of Righteousness Evangelistic Ministries
Founder/Executive Director of the
Anointed To Be Kings Male Mentoring Program

ACKNOWLEDGEMENTS

To my God fearing husband Pastor Jonathan, thanks for your unconditional love as you assist me into becoming what God has called me to be. Your faith in me has catapulted me to live life with no limitations, your wisdom and knowledge of His Word is still an inspiration even after being married for 11 years. Your ability to keep God present in all that you say or do has helped me to always be conscience of who He is, I thank you for all you do to add to the anointing that's on my life, and I thank you for sharing the anointing that's on yours. Love you forever, you are truly amazing!

To my best friend Minister Norma Gonzalez, I have discovered through my walk with God that there are people who come into your life for a short term and there are those that God sends into your life to help you reach your divine destiny. You have helped me to see that there is such a thing as true friendships with long lasting power. You are definitely a provisional relationship from God and I thank Him daily for giving me the opportunity to experience a divine friendship, your unconditional love as well as the ongoing support that you give to assist me in my call. Love you forever and looking forward to continuing our partnership in ministry.

To my spiritual father Dr. Abraham E. Fenton an end time Apostle of God. I thank you for your willingness to assist me in doing the work that our Father has called me too. Just being afforded the opportunity to sit at your feet and learn with clarity the true gospel of Jesus Christ. The wisdom that you so willingly share and guidance you so graciously give helps me to stay focus and keeps me looking straight ahead. Thanks for sharing with Jonathan and I your ministry gifts.

To the Board Members of "Women Walking in the Spirit Ministries" Sister Dawn Jones, Sister Doreen Milton, Sister Sabreen Harris & my best friend Minister Norma Gonzalez. All of you have played a significant role in my life as well as the ministry, I thank God for our friendships and that He saw fit to hand pick each of you to assist me in *"saving a life, one child at a time!"*

PREFACE

It's ever so often that I look back over the years to recognize God and give Him all the glory and honor for what He has done, and continues to do in my life. I also can't begin to thank all the many people He has used to help me to arrive at this place in my life. I'm in awe over my salvation, and honestly I find it an honor as well as a privilege to know God, and be used by Him to impact the lives of so many. Years ago I accepted the fact that I could do nothing to repay Him for His unmerited favor, nor for His empowering presence in my life. In appreciation toward God, I've made a conscious effort to pour out my life on the altar and make every effort to be all that He has created me to be in hopes of my life bringing glory to His Name.

It was probably close to two years ago that I began writing this book, I actually had another topic in mind but as I continued to seek God for direction concerning what to write, this is what I believe He wanted me to share. Throughout ***"In Love Under New Management"*** you will discover who Gwendolyn Ann Cook is, the trials that she has encountered and the blessings she has received. I'm not content with keeping to myself what I have endured, if by chance by allowing you into my world it will help you, then so be it.

I've discovered that what little I know, it's truly my desire for others to know as well. I find it necessary to be open and transparent especially in regards to those God has entrusted in my care.

As you read *"In Love Under New Management"* you'll discover that I have not always been pleasing in the sight of God, and sometimes I even fall short today. I thank Him daily for His grace and mercies, and the knowledge that if not for His love I would definitely not be alive today. No matter how good or bad your life is, every circumstance can change for the best as you purpose to trust in Him, leaving no room for doubt as you discover to know a **"Love that's eternal."**

My prayer is that as you read this book you too will fall *"In Love Under New Management."*

Gwendolyn Ann Cook

INTRODUCTION

"The best way to predict the future is to create it!"
Author Unknown

Thank you for purchasing my book! I'm truly grateful for your trust in me; it is my prayer that the investment of your money and time in yourself will inspire you to reach new heights as you set new goals and remove all barriers.

For those of you who may not have any idea of who I am or even why I see fit to try and inspire you. Allow me to introduce myself, the name given to me at birth was "Gwendolyn Ann Greene" at the young age of forty-six I fell in love *(I believe for the first time in my life)* and married the love of my life, and became "Gwendolyn Ann Cook." Prior to my meeting Jonathan, I had never been involved in a substantial relationship, I thank God that I considered myself prior to my marriage to be complete in my singleness.

Although I was born into a Christian family, I lost sight of that when I was old enough to make a decision on whether or not I continued to go to Church. In 1982 I endured a number of challenges with my health, one being an issue of blood which provoked me to run right into the arms of God. It seemed as though immediately the things that I once loved

I began to hate, and the things that I once thought I hated I began to love.

Although as quiet as it was kept, most of my life I lived with a very low self-image of myself. I've always had an issue with my weight and struggled for years trying to lose it with little to no success. As I got older I decided that there was definitely no chance of me ever being a "brickhouse" 36-24-36! As I came to except that, I began to turn my focus off of me on to others who I thought I could assist in living out their dreams. While doing that I discovered this quote and used it not only for others but for myself as well.

> ***"Wake up and dream! Dream bigger than your imagination can imagine…Then pursue it!"***
>
> -JAT

Many of you may be familiar with the books title, ***In Love Under New Management,*** a song made popular by Miki Howard. Although a secular song the words could easily explain how someone very special came into my life and filled the empty space, that would be Jesus, and today I can proclaim that my life has been changed. I'm here to tell you if it happened for me it can happen for you.

As you read ***"In Love Under New Management"*** you will discover that I haven't always been pleasing in the sight of God, after many years of frustration and disappointments through the power of God I experienced an unconditional surrender and chose to make a difference in my life and the lives of others. You'll discover how God is using me to impact the lives of our misdirected youth-at-risk, and to bring recovery to communities in need of an economic development.

I pray that through the contents of this book you will allow God to lead you to fall ***"In Love Under New Management."*** My earnest prayer is that it will cause a domino effect in the lives of all of whom you have the ability to influence.

For ever since the creation of the world His invisible nature and attributes, that is. His eternal power and divinity have been made intelligible and clearly discernible in and through the things that have been made (His handiworks). So [men] are without excuse [altogether without any defense or justification], [Ps. 19.1-4.]

(Romans 1:20, Amp.)

CHAPTER 1

Unconditional Surrender!

I truly believe that the Spirit of God wants us to progress, but He's not going to force you forward. So it just may be time for you to do a turn around and reconnect. If we are to get disentangled from the web of sinful attitudes and/or actions, we must be absolutely honest with ourselves and with the Lord. If you cannot truthfully see any progress toward Christlikeness in your character, it may be time for you to make a U-turn, and unconditionally surrender. First we must accept total responsibility for ourselves and our actions. How can we expect to be all that God has called us to be unless we first take responsibility for our behavior? On the other

Gwendolyn Ann Cook

hand, self-destructive behaviors and habits can cause you to become your own worst enemy. God wants to deliver us from self-defeating emotions and thought patterns, such as internal self-pity, low self-esteem, self-righteousness, judgmentalism, unrestrained anger, un-forgiveness, idolatry, envy, jealousy, selfishness, fear, and possessing a critical spirit. These things not only grieve the Holy Spirit but have the potential to cause pain to you and to those around you. If the Bible teaches anything, it is personal accountability.

One of the most challenging changes for me was to stop making excuses or trying to justify my own self-serving actions. In life, we are responsible for what we do and/or what we choose to be involved with. One day for sure we will give an account to God for it. It's either "yes" to God with no fine print in the contract, or it's "no." You don't grow into a right relationship with God, much less drift into it. You must deliberately step into it by faith. Satan knows what God intends for you, and he will do anything to keep you from getting there. He knows that you have legitimate needs, which seemingly at times are not being met. He will use your frustration by causing you to live independently of God. By means of deception countless people learn to live in denial. In time most people come to rely on their own ability rather than God's. Yet despite the tendency to lean on our flesh, by virtue of God's grace we have victory in Christ. The good news is that what He reveals, He also heals. Psalm 147:3 says, *"He heals the brokenhearted, and binds up their wounds."* However, when a wound on your body heals, there may be a scar remaining as a reminder, but it's no longer painful. When Jesus the Christ heals the wounds of our heart, the memory

2

no longer throbs with painful thoughts. It will no longer yield a spirit of depression, oppression or suppression. God not only intends for you to be saved but He also desires for you to enjoy life to the fullest. John 10:10 confirms this thought, *"I am come that they might have life, and that they might have it more abundantly."*

As you read this book it is my hope that you sense God pulling you closer to Himself. He wants to pull you out of your yesterday, to prepare you for tomorrow while supernaturally manifesting Himself in your present situation. So to be totally transformed with a lasting change, you need to be unconditionally surrendered consumed with desire for His presence. God is calling each of us to total submission and into an intimate relationship with Him. No matter how discouraged you may be or how hopeless your life appears in the present, your God has made promises to you and you can't give up without seeing them come to past.

Believe it or not everything that I tried to do in the flesh has ended in failure, causing me to fall far short of God's glory. Not until I surrendered to the Spirit of God have I been able to start as well as finish a task or goal. I spent many years looking for love in all the wrong places; I'm not speaking about sexual relationships alone. For many years I found myself doing things I didn't even like while attempting to discover who I was, as well as my purpose in life. I worked at jobs I didn't even enjoy for years despite dreading to go to work every day, I did not have enough self-esteem to search out other employment opportunities. I had girlfriends and associates I hung out with that I knew that were not in any position to add anything positive to my life. I continued in those relationships knowing that they lacked good character qualities and that their lack of integrity was eventually going to rub off on me, and it did.

I knew deep inside that God had something better for me, so I set out to discover it. I was raised in Church and even as a little girl I use to sit outside my grandmothers prayer closet and listen to her pray and re-act to the presence of the Holy Spirit falling on her. My cousins seem to think it was funny for momma (*what we called our grand-mother*) to be speaking in a funny language, not me; I thought it was amazing for her to speak in Spanish (*tongues*) being that we were African American. I knew then that I had a special connection with her; even though she has gone home to be with the Lord, I now understand that what we had was a spiritual connection.

When You Get Sick and Tired of Being Sick and Tired!

After many years of frustration and running into so many brick walls and people who were definitely unworthy of my love or even friendship, which left me most often with nothing but hurt feelings, it was time to make a change in my life. I needed someone to cling to, someone who would love me unconditionally. Yes, I had an awesome pair of parents who made sure I did not have a need for anything. Siblings who loved me in their own special way, especially my sister Niecy, she loved everyone and everything. Niecy, still today is extremely caring and protective of me. Without any intentions to hurt my other siblings feeling, Niecy has always been my favorite because she too had unconditional love for me.

God was showing me that sometimes our faith is perfected more so when things don't change than when they do. You don't need faith for what you can see or for what you already have. You need faith when no answer has come yet, when life makes no sense, when you can't explain or understand any of it. The awesome thing is that God Himself will never leave you alone, He will be right there, through every trial with you, coaching, teaching and sometimes even carrying you, *"I am with you and will watch over you wherever you go, and I will bring you back to this land. I will not leave you until I have done what I have promised you"* (Genesis 28:15).

Experiencing God's love is a choice that results in action; He chose to love us and sent Jesus to die for us when we were still yet sinners, *"Christ died for us while we were still sinners"* (Romans 5:8), this demonstrates God's unconditional love for us. We should never forget that! He just made up His mind to do it. I can clearly remember the day that I surrendered, my mind was made up and I finally discovered the new love of my life and His name is Jesus! Are you ready to make the great turnaround? Do it now! It's time to experience, ***"In Love Under New Management."***

My Sister Niecy!

"For we ourselves were once foolish, disobedient, led astray, slaves to various passions and pleasures, passing our days in malice and envy, hated by others and hating one another. But when the goodness and loving kindness of God our Savior appeared, he saved us, not because of works done by us in righteousness, but according to his own mercy by the washing of regeneration and renewal of the Holy Spirit, whom he poured out on us richly through Jesus Christ our Savior, so that being justified by his grace we might become heirs according to the hope of eternal life."

(Titus 3:3-7, ESV)

CHAPTER 2

A Personal Revival!

God can speak to us and when He does we must know His timing. In knowing the timing of God it will cause us to be a person of both discipline and of patience. Our heavenly Father desires to communicate with us even more than we desire to communicate with Him. You see, He knows where we are spiritually and will speak to us accordingly. His Word comes to us in various ways, the Prophet Jeremiah prophesied, *"Is not my word like a fire? Saith the Lord; and like a hammer that breaketh the rock in pieces?"* (Jerimiah 23:29). Therefore, the Word of God can be powerfully directed to us like a fire, or like a hammer breaking down all opposition. The Holy Spirit is able to develop our spiritual sensitivity whereby we are able to test what we hear, distinguishing between God's voice and the voice of another. We must learn to silence the strange voices in order to hear the voice of God. Then and only then will we know what God would have us to do and the steps He would have us to take.

Time for a Personal Revival!

In the year of 1996, I could sense in my spirit that God was leading me into a season of personal revival. Revival is a time when Christians are revived or restored to their first love for Christ, when shame and hypocrisy are exposed; when bitterness and strife exist in the body of Christ are revealed and repented of under the guidance of the Holy Spirit's convicting power; a time when such changes are impacted in the lives of Christians, a time when sinners are brought to Christ in great numbers. Revival is when spiritual vitality is visible to others and leads to a change in them, which is seen both in a spreading renewal among believers and a turning to Christ among unbelievers. At this time I became a force to be reckoned with, what I was experiencing internally was clearly seen externally in my behavior. I no longer talked like I use to especially when it came to using filthy words. My personal revival provoked me to make a drastic change in the way that I had been living, even to the point of what I no longer desired to watch on television. The music I used to listen to was no longer pleasing to my ear, I wanted to hear music that would give God glory and at the same time lift my spirit. I hadn't realized the shift until it was brought to my attention. The way I dressed drastically changed because I was used to showing what was legally acceptable to be revealed in public. My dress attire soon became modest to complement my spoken words and my new desire to represent my Lord and Savior Jesus Christ; I walked into a season of transformation. Scripture says, in 2 Corinthians 3:18, *"And we all, who with unveiled faces contemplate the Lord's glory, are being transformed into his image with ever-increasing glory, which comes from the Lord, who is the Spirit."* The real ministry of life is to help others realize how to behold Christ in an unveiled way as to mirror Him as we are transformed into His image. The more we behold Him, the more we reflect Him and are transformed into His image. The longer we as the mirrors behold Christ, the more we are transformed into His image in order to become a full reflection of His goodness. This definitely is not a matter of your gift, teaching, or knowledge; it is a matter of the life of Christ living within you. The new man is the workmanship of God, born of the Spirit, and has the Spirit of Christ dwelling in him. When Christ returns we are to be conformed into His image, the image of His glory. We shall be glorified together with Him because we are predestined to be conformed to His image. Through my personal revival I came to truly believe the Scripture found in 2 Corinthians 5:17 where it says, *"Therefore, if anyone is in Christ, he is a new creation. The old has passed away; behold, the new has come."*

I had begun to lose friends due to my letting go of the old and entering into the newness of life in order to experience true transformation. In order to experience a personal revival;

one must first believe in the redemptive work of our Lord Jesus Christ which was done for us on the cross. What Christ came to do is complete. We all must ask God to open our eyes and enlighten our minds through the Holy Spirit so that we will be able to have a deeper and better understanding of the whole truth of the gospel. We have to make an effort to live in greater dependence on God the Father with a renewed mind to live our lives from the fullness of that which God the Father gave us in Jesus Christ. Life is surely a battleground, and should definitely not be considered a playground, it took me to become a woman of resolution with a made up mind to face the enemy and win the battle. I had determined in my heart that from this time forward I would obey God and please Him, no matter what the cost or what the lost. I found it to be a privilege to strive toward being a "transformer" and not a "conformer." It is a process, and I am far from the goal, but I do desire to present my body as a living and holy sacrifice, *"So here's what I want to do, God helping you: Take your everyday, ordinary life – your sleeping, eating, going-to-work, and walking-around life – and place it before God as an offering. Embracing what God does for you is the best thing you can do for him. Don't become so well-adjusted to your culture that you fit into it without even thinking. Instead, fix your attention on God. You'll be changed from the inside out. Readily recognize what he wants from you, and quickly respond to it. Unlike the culture around you, develops well-formed maturity in you"* (Romans 12:1-2, MSG). It is, in reality a day-by-day commitment to persevere in God's strength, and not my own. I find myself desiring more than ever to be all that God wants me to be. We are marvelously privileged to be saved by grace and loved to the extent that the Spirit abides within us to guide us and teach us how to live. By grace, we are being shown how to turn our backs on a godless, self-indulgent life, and how to take on a God-filled, God-honoring life. In making a decision to live according to the standards of God I chose to be resolute by taking a stand for righteousness moving from a life full of defeat to a life of victory. Through the joy of building godly character, I have learned to deal with the difficulties that sometimes confront me.

for I know the plans that I have for you, 'declares the Lord, 'plans for welfare and not for calamity to give you a future and a hope. Then you will call upon Me and come and pray to Me, and I will listen to you. And you will seek Me and find Me, when you search for Me with all your heart."

(Jeremiah 29:11-13)

CHAPTER 3

The Importance of Knowing Your Purpose

When we come to know the purpose and the plan that God has placed in us prior to our birth, we then can begin to live a life endowed with His grace. Jesus told us that in the world we would have tribulation, and certainly we do. I think the key is trusting God enough to be content in the knowledge that He knows what is best for each situation. I find it extremely interesting that God Himself sent the thorn to Paul to keep him from being prideful. In 2 Corinthians 12:8, he warns the believers to be careful about thinking of themselves more highly than they should. If it is not helpful for the "thorn" to be removed, then I must then believe that enduring the thorn in the sufficiency of grace is for my good.

In living out your purpose and walking in it, the enemy will often raise his little ugly head.

I have come to the understanding that the world equates weakness with failure. It is only by the grace of God that we are enabled to say, that when we are weak, we are strong. His grace is what makes us content with weakness, and only through grace can the power of Christ dwell in us. Being recipients of God's super abounding grace, having the liberty to love and serve, and having the divine enablement to live godly lives we need to be in the process of being known as men and women of purpose as well as men and women of grace. If you have not discovered your God given purpose the enemy will discover one for you.

I grew up struggling with my weight which led me as a teenager to become a closet eater; I was too embarrassed to eat publically. I recall people often saying to me that I had such a cute face, maybe you should lose some weight it would really help you to look better, (*can you believe that*). At the age of twenty-one a male close friend who happen to have been a homosexual told me about pills that would help me lose weight fast, he told me I could buy them in Camden, NJ on Federal Street. Not knowing much about Camden at the time he informed me that he had a cousin who lived in Camden that would happily get them for me. I gave him the money and a couple days later he showed up at my house with the pills. He said the name of the pills was *black beauties,* and he also stated that I needed to make sure I ate something when I begin taking them.

That same day I began taking the black pills and in less than a week I had lost close to fifteen pounds, with such a drastic weight lost in what I believed to have been such a short time I now began to focus on my appearance. I began to buy new clothes that would complement my desired size; I had been losing five to ten pounds a week. Within thirty days I had lost over forty pounds and on my way to becoming a brick house which was often my confession! After using the black beauties purchased for me from the streets of Camden I found a legal way to acquire the same pills from a doctor's office in Burlington, NJ on High Street. The doctor was extremely popular, and you didn't have to make an appointment. All you needed was thirty-five dollars and a lot of time, most visits due to the demand as well as his clientell would take several hours of waiting. I would take the pills accompanied with a diuretic, lose the desired weight and after a few weeks stop going for a while until I regained the weight lost, and then I would start going back again. For years I did the same thing over and over again trying to be known for someone other than just having a pretty face. Myself, as well as many other believers have discovered that their biggest adversary is the spirit of deception. Because from the time you took your first breath of air, the devil has been subtly trying to molest your soul through deception. The reason for his persistence is that he knows that the best way to hurt God, whom he hates, is to hurt you, a child of God. Satan knows that your Heavenly Father has a good plan for your life, a plan with purpose and a divine destiny, and he doesn't want you to experience it.

Who's Influencing You?

So few women are aware that they are constantly being influenced by what other people say or by thoughts planted in their minds by the devil. Like myself you could be led away from the truth without even knowing it, by television programs you find yourself watching, music you listen to, or what you happen to read or see on the internet, places you go or even by those you choose to associate with. These things may not seem so important to you at the time, but the truth is that every choice you make is significant, and every choice you make ultimately will affect you spiritually, either for good or for evil. Before discovering my purpose I allowed the dictates of this world to bring definition to my life; I lived a life only pleasing to others, because it wasn't even pleasing to me. After losing the weight I dressed in a way that was indecent as well as trifling, the more I revealed made me feel the most attractive. I allowed myself to be described as someone with a filthy mouth; my vocabulary was extremely limited to mostly four letter words. I could out cuss a sailor any time of day, I found myself not loving anyone not even myself. This made it easy for me to get involved with other women's husbands. I made it a point only to date married men, so that after I got all I could from them (*mainly money which is a form of prostitution*) I could easily move on to the next one. I didn't exactly date them anyway, I was dating their possessions. So if you didn't have anything you didn't have me. Back then I was fascinated with luxury cars, I often dated a man based on the car he drove. My favorite car was the Jaguar, so if you had a Jaguar and other noticeable possession regardless of your looks or lack of character you could easily have had me sitting in your front passenger's seat or driving your car. (***Today I presently own a Jaguar by the grace of God***).

Eventually in time, I came face to face with the part of me that I so often tried to keep hidden. The things about me which I found to be unacceptable or even ugly I had to take an honest look at all aspects of it in the face, and learn by the grace of God to accept them. In doing so I found that the ugliness was a figment of an ungodly imagination, something that I along with others helped to create. Philippians 4:8-9 Message Bible says this about what we are to think about and imagine, *"Summing it all up, friends, I'd say you'll do best by filling your minds and meditating on things true, noble, reputable, authentic, compelling, gracious, the best, not the worst; the beautiful, not the ugly; things to praise, not things to curse."* Our true beauty is what shines within, and once we realize that we have been molded like that of clay by our Creator we then can begin to love ourselves, and purpose in our hearts to become the person that He has created us to be.

As one who oversees a mentoring program for Youth-At-Risk females I have discovered through our counseling sessions that this is how a lot of our young girls as well as many grown women think today. Many will, and have sold their souls to the devil in order to obtain things. Believe it or not I had never heard of anyone spiritual or secular speaking of mentoring as I was growing up, definitely not in a positive way. And like today many of our elders are trying hard at making a living that there is no time available to spend with someone younger in hopes of helping them to live a successful life.

Today I am the Founder/President of a "Female Youth-At-Risk Mentoring Program." My purpose is to devote a great deal of time and effort to help young women and teenage girls to discover their God given purpose. The Program is a female only organization designed for women as well as youth with behavioral issues and/or those desiring to have someone assist them in fulfilling their God ordained assignment. Special emphasis is placed on assisting teenage females who are presently in an Alternative School setting and for teenaged girls who are incarcerated. The Program offers certified training for women and young female adults who desire to be used by God in impacting the lives of others. Individual mentoring is provided for the incarcerated mentee's with the hope of helping to prepare them for their re-entry back into the community after the completion of their sentence. Those who are accepted as mentee's are assigned mentors who are trained and educated by myself as well as my own mentor Rev. Dr. Eve Lynne Fenton, who is Founder & President of "Women In Covenant." The mentors are assigned to meet the needs of their mentee and will continue until they no longer require or desire mentorship.

I believe if I had someone speaking into my life like a mentor when I was living a misdirected life I possibly would have avoided many of the brick walls that brought with it discouragement and many years of disappointment. This is why I try extremely hard to be a pillar in the community for women and young girls. I find it to be fulfilling when I can help and assist women and young girls bound by the spirit of prostitution and/or drug addiction in Camden, as well as throughout Southern New Jersey and those that we mentor in the Northern parts of Jersey. I don't believe if given a choice these women or young girls would sell their bodies for little to nothing and spend many cold lonely nights sleeping with strangers or on the streets possibly in a dumpster. I believe it is important to help them discover their God given purpose, in turn by doing so we provoke them to live a lifestyle pleasing to God.

With being an overseer of a "women's ministry" one of the burdens that God has placed on my heart is to minister to women who live a life prostituting their bodies. You can often find me walking the streets of Camden, N.J. in hopes of encountering women who may be sick and tired of the lifestyle, and are ready to be delivered from the addictions that have brought them to such a low self-image. I recall one Saturday afternoon myself along with Pastors Ayanna Moore and Rebecca Caldwell took love to the streets by stopping several women on the corner of Broadway and Spruce sharing the love of God. I even found myself sitting down on the sidewalk with them listening to how they ended up living a self-destructive life, prostituting with an addiction to heroin and/or crack. This was even filmed and can be seen in a documentary entitled "Kids are dying" by Michael Deleon. All but one of the young women was Caucasian, the one being African American. A majority of the women that we encounter on the streets are Caucasian in a predominately African American community. Our purpose was to help them come to the saving knowledge of our Savior Jesus Christ. Little did we know that five (5) out of all the women we ministered to that day were ready and willing to come in off the streets and go into a detox facility.

Bound by the spirit of prostitution!

***Real ministry is when you can knock the walls down
of your church and confront the spirits that
have so many in our communities bound.***

I have to admit that I did not have a plan in place if this sort of thing was to happen, so my husband who was there ministering alongside of us started making calls in hopes of finding a detox facility. We eventually discovered that Camden even though over the years has earned the title of being the poorest city in the Nation along with ranking #1 in crime in America, presently has no detox facilities. We continued to search out programs however, with no avail; every facility that he called said that they would only take them if they had health insurance. ***You might have to help me understand this one, how in the world could a State funded organization possibly think that someone who's prostituting on the streets, addicted to heroin and/or crack would maintain their health insurance benefits.***

With me not willing to release these women back into the streets I thought to reach out to Mayor Dana Redd who was a friend and the Mayor of Camden City. While awaiting information from her staff we gathered the women in our cars and transported them to the Social Services Office on Broadway and Market Street in Camden. Due to the lateness of the hour they were unable to assist us until Monday with this being late on Friday. Pastor Jonathan was able to reach a man of God who he had recently come in contact with, after being introduced by one of our church members. The Pastor was the overseer of a drug rehab facility *(Joshua Achievement Center)* in Philly; they were able to interview the women and process them over the phone and they were also willing to receive them into their facility, but not until Monday morning. Then all we needed at this point was a place for them to stay until Monday.

Sometimes you have to feed them, physically as well as spiritually!

We sensed that they were hungry being that we had been out on the streets already for over five (5) hours; we ended up taking them to a restaurant to get something to eat while waiting for a response to what could be done with them before they changed their minds and were no longer willing to accept our help. With the assistance of the Mayor's office the door was opened to take them to a shelter in the City for the weekend and plans were then made for Pastor Jonathan and I to transport them to the *Joshua Achievement Center* in Philadelphia on Monday as agreed. I had told two of the women that I would reach out to their family members to tell them their condition and to share with them the decision they made to enter into a substance abuse program. Neither one of these two (2) young women were residents of the city of Camden, one was from Blackwood and the other from Mantua, New Jersey. When I returned home that Friday night I called the number given to me by one of the women, a man answered the phone; I began to share with him that my husband and I are Pastors who do outreach ministry on the streets of Camden, New Jersey. I then told him that I had encountered a young woman who I believe to be his daughter on the streets, and she has made the decision to get help. The man said he was her father and began crying and screaming loudly in my ear, I held the phone back from my ear and listened to him give thanks to Jesus for his daughter's life. The next voice I heard was a female, who said she was her mother, she then went on to share with me that they had not heard from their daughter in over a year, she said that they thought she was possibly dead. She began to tell me that she and her husband had custody of her two (2) year old daughter and she too has not seen her mother for over a year. The father apparently regained his composure and got back on the phone and thanked me for helping their daughter, he said that she has been addicted to heroin for some time now and that is why they have taken custody of their granddaughter.

When Monday came we went to the women's shelter in Camden to retrieve the women and the staff reported to us that the women left Saturday morning and did not return, they even left the few belongings they had with them. You know how the enemy shows up and begins whispering in your ear, *well he began to remind me of where these women came from and that the time that we invested in them was wasted.* I have to admit that I did have some concerns about leaving them in the City with no supervision or a support system to help them over the weekend. I knew that there was a strong possibility for them to feel a need to go looking for a John to assist them in acquiring money to fund their addiction. I began to call the numbers we were given and got no answer, suddenly a call came in from an unknown number, I answered and it was one of the young women calling from a John's cell phone. She shared that her and another woman had a disagreement and she decided to leave the shelter. However, despite what took place she said that she was still ready to go to the rehab facility. We told her that we were parked on Broadway across from the transportation center. In response, believe it or not her John brought her to us. Shortly after meeting with her the other young women called and said that she was on her way back to the shelter to retrieve her belongings; she also went on to say that she stayed in North Camden overnight. We connected with two of the five (5) young women and decided to take them to visit their families before we admitted them into the rehab facility in Philly. It was truly a blessing to see the face of one of the young woman's daughter when she saw her mother get out of our car; also the looks on her parents face as well.

Next time you run into a woman who appears to be bound by the spirit of prostitution take the time to ask her if given a choice would she still choose this profession, ask her!

I find it to be real ministry when you can knock the walls down of your church and confront the spirits that have so many in our communities bound. I believe that we can no longer allow the lost to stay lost; we cannot be content with so many people remaining in darkness. We can no longer sit back and leave it to the male man, Jesus Himself has liberated women and yet in this society we keep going back to the old ways, this is not the time to be timid or lackadaisical regarding the lives of so many people. Did you know that the first redemptive promise found in the Word of God is that although Satan would bruise the heel of her seed, her seed would crush the head of Satan? (Gen. 3:15). I think this is an incredible redemptive promise. It is shameful that the adversary has so many believing women cowering in fear, losing sight of the fact that their seed will one day crush the enemy's head. It's time for the women of God to shake off the bruising that you may see and even feel at times and begin to confess that the heels of your physical and your spiritual sons and daughters will someday crush the enemy's head. We have to stop struggling and come to the understanding of who we are in Christ. Men, as well as women, who are made in the image of God and His likeness, share a unique position and relationship in God. In Genesis 1:28, God gave two commandments to the first couple, *"And God blessed them and said to them, Be fruitful, multiply, and fill the earth, and subdue it [using all its vast resources in the service of God and man]; and have dominion over the fish of the sea, the birds of the air, and over every living creature that moves upon the earth."*

Listen to me reader! It is of the utmost importance that we understand the women in this (*new place*) to which the Lord Jesus Christ is calling us to. God wants us to come to the place where we will never look back. God has no room for the person who looks back, thinks back, or acts back. It's time for you to rise up and initiate the plan of God.

When you don't know who you are!
-Drug Addiction/Prostitution-

Pastors Jonathan W. & Gwendolyn Ann Cook
Soul Winners

"For I reckon that the sufferings of this present time are not worthy to be compared with the glory which shall be revealed in us."

(Romans 8:18, KJV)

CHAPTER 4

When You Don't Know Who You Are!

I was born into a military family; we often traveled due to my father's status. At the age of 13 in the year of 1971 our family was relocated to Fort Dix, New Jersey from Fort Campbell, Kentucky. I grew up in a home that openly expressed love toward one another. I was one (1) of five siblings and the youngest at that. My late father, who is now spending eternity in heaven, was a member of the United States Army. He was a tall dark skinned man with extremely broad shoulders and a strong looking body stature. My dad also had high cheek bones and other attractive features which made him very pleasant to look at. He was what you would call handsome and distinguished all at the same time. To see daddy in his uniform even as a young girl made me very proud to be his daughter, everyone who knew him appeared to have had a great deal of respect for him.

Being the youngest I was of course daddy's little girl in age but definitely not in size. My sisters and my brother classified me as being spoiled rotten. At a young age I had a weight problem and my siblings often called me names other than the name on my birth certificate. This is one of the reasons why I believe daddy showed me special attention, helping me to take the focus off of what they were saying. In doing that he always found a way to make me feel pretty, he always would say that I was such a beautiful little girl. *Daddy would say that they were just jealous because God gave me so much beauty that they couldn't handle it.* He also said that one day they too would see the beauty in me and they would stop calling me all those ugly names. Daddy would often tell me to tell them that *"sticks and stones may break my bones but names will never hurt me."* He didn't know that I would rather have had the sticks and the stones, knowing that the outside bruises would eventually go away. But the words landed deep down in my soul and the wounds they caused stayed with me for many years. His side of the family would often say when they saw me that I looked like his late mother. There was only one picture that I remembered seeing of my grandmother Genève and in it I could not see the resemblance. I recall his youngest sister named Betty, who treated me special as well, she looked like she may have been Indian; I had often heard family members say that Indian blood ran in our family on my father's side. Aunt Betty was my favorite aunt, as a little girl she often brought me gifts when she came to visit.

As I became older I still couldn't see myself as being pretty, even as a teenager I always felt out of place everywhere I went. My three (3) sisters grew up to be so beautiful in their own right. They developed into very attractive young ladies. Here I am, by the way still struggling with the issue of weight. I remember when they would; including my brother at times out of anger calling me names like "Porky the pig, Bessie the cow, and Arnold ziffol." Arnold was the pig who had a staring role on the sitcom Green Acres. I would cry when they did that and run to my dad, even in my late teens he would comfort me by taking me out to eat.

Sergeant Major George Albert Greene
Daddy
December 19, 1929 – April 11, 2005

I recall some of my eight grade classmates who also suffered from some form of identity crises, whether it was weight or a facial feature that they didn't feel good about; or some other thing which caused a very low self-esteem. We were graduating and preparing ourselves for Jr. High. I guess in the eight grade I had a few good friends because we all kind of felt unworthy. We were fearful of what was ahead of us, and that was ninth graders, we heard that on our first day we would have to experience initiation. Already we were trying to deal with our own issues, and now these ninth graders are going to pounce on us and call us out of our names.

When They Don't Know Who You Are!

In the ninth grade I had it hard; since my father was in the Army we lived on the Fort Dix Military Base. A great many of the other kids were from a community called "Lake Valley Acres." These kids, speaking of the girls were vicious towards me, for some reason a large number of them wanted to abuse me daily. My teachers especially Mrs. Jenkins would express encouragement by telling me that they were just jealous because they knew I was going to make something of my life and they weren't. I fought my way out of middle school into high school. Just about every day when the bell rang at the end of the school day, several of them would follow me to my bus calling me distasteful names and sticking pins in me, saying that they were releasing the air out of my fat body. Now, I did not want to fight but often times I had to. I was definitely not a punk, but because of their actions they provoked me to be confrontational, so I went head to toe with the best of them. Today some of these same girls who are now grown women, God has opened the door for me to lead them to the Lord; one of them even participated in my wedding.

It amazes me how Scripture has a way of speaking to every situation that you may experience in your life, the Word of God says, *"But God has chosen the foolish things of the world, that he may put to shame the wise; and God has chosen the weak things of the world, that he may put to shame the strong things"* (1 Corinthians 1:27, DBT).

"The path of the just is as the shining light, that shineth more and more unto the perfect day." Therefore, I continue to seek to see myself, and the world around me, through the eyes of my Father in Heaven, and to help others do the same."

(Proverbs 4:18)

CHAPTER 5

Suffering from an Identity Crisis

So often due to the ministry I oversee, I run into women and even teenage girls who are struggling with an identity crisis. One woman in particular my husband and I met as we were preparing to relocate from a house to a Condo. We met this young woman at a self-storage facility who ended up assisting us in procuring a storage unit for our household goods. Immediately upon entering the store I could see that she was dealing with her identity due to her appearance as well as her masculine mannerisms. I felt along with my husband the need to pray with her; after procuring a storage unit we were compelled to minister the Gospel of Jesus Christ. Before we left the store we prayed and invited her to come to Church with us on the upcoming Sunday. Although she tried very hard not to accept the invitation I would not, nor would my husband Jonathan take no for an answer. She immediately insisted that she had nothing to wear to a Church service and stated that she was not interested in organized religion; I assured her that she could come as she was and God Himself is definitely not into organized religion.

Sunday came and the three (3) of us arrived at Church, even though I could tell she felt very uncomfortable I tried my best to reassure her that she was in fact going to receive a blessing from God. During the service I could see that she was getting involved in the message, at the end of service as the Pastor proposed the altar call, I noticed her rising to her feet and heading toward the altar. That day she became a citizen of the Kingdom of Heaven. Shortly after, she joined the Church and following the completion of her probationary period she had a strong desire to get more involved in the ministry not only as one who attends, but to become a servant in the body of Christ. I continued to make myself available to her as she prepared to live a life pleasing in the sight of God. I watched her in Church doing what she could to fit in, even though her masculine mannerism and the be-bop in her walk were hard to overlook.

Several years later I had the opportunity to encounter this woman again, the proclamation of her deliverance was loud and bold even though the masculine mannerism was still present along with the be-bop in her walk. Upon being reconnected I recall her telling me that I had been such an influence in her early walk with the Lord, she even shared that I was like a mother to her, and began to call me her mom on several occasions. Believe it or not this caused a red flag to rise. She had been absent from my life for more than seven (7) years, even while members of the same Church contact was lost due to the direction I was going in. As our relationship was being re-established I was compelled to assist her in discovering her freedom. She informed me that she was interested in writing a book and did not know where to begin. Since I was a successful published author of two (2) books and having had assisted several new authors in publishing their stories I agreed to assist her in publishing hers. One thing I knew for sure was that I was not put into her life to judge her, my position was to be the extension of God's hand and love on her. God loves each and every one of us and He died to rescue us from all sin, even homosexuality. It was obvious that we had little to nothing in common except the fact that we were both born females. God distributes gifts and one of the areas that He has gifted me in is how to love people who have lifestyles that are in direct contrast to the way I live and what I believe. There is no heart that can love like the heart that God has touched, the love that is made to love the sinner. We must always be in a transforming position and not in a conforming condition, whereas we are always renewing our mind and being consistedly renovated by the mighty thoughts of God, being brought into line with what God has said to us by the Spirit. *"This is the way, walk in it"* (Isaiah 30:21). *"Walk in the Spirit, and you shall not fulfill the lust of the flesh"* (Galatians 5:16).

I've been asked on several occasions how do you minister to a person when presented with the homosexuality of a family member, friend or even a co-worker, as well as one of your neighbors. Believe it or not most often that spirit has been revealed even prior to the announcement being made; I can assure you that it can be an extremely tense conversation for all involved. That's why I believe it is so important for the Church to be prepared for the onslaught of this diabolical spirit. If ministry in this area is not guided by the Holy Spirit many lost in this sin may be provoked to turn to and strongly embrace the homosexual community. Many may feel that this is the only place left for them to obtain love and acceptance. Another important fact we must know and always remember that it is not our job to make or try to force someone back to a heterosexual lifestyle. Move out of the way and allow the Master to work; as His vessels we just have to keep the lines of communication open.

Being Used By God!

While employed for over twenty (20) years as a civilian on a Military Base I have come to know a little something about women as well as men suffering from an identity crisis. During my tenure working for the United States Armed Forces I became acquainted with several female soldiers who classified themselves as being gay or lesbians hiding their sin in the closet. However the female soldiers knew from the front door that I did not swing that way and I was definitely strictly interested in the male population, *(possibly too interested).* Through the years I witnessed many of them get so far away that I often wondered how they were ever going to find their way back. When I look back over my life I can see how God even in my own tailored made sin saw fit to use me as one of His agents.

I can recall my first encounter with a young boy with whom I attended high school with even in his early teens, not only dressed in the appearance of a female but also considered he himself female as well. A few years later I heard that he had transgender surgery to become a complete female. I remember receiving an announcement regarding his upcoming marriage to a prominent business man in Philadelphia. Back then in the early seventies a large majority of me and my sisters Joy and Niecy had many close friends who were homosexuals. I can remember the pain in my chest of hearing the passing of at least three of them who die of the Aids virus. It was definitely nothing new to me to befriend males who desired to be a female.

One of the members of the Officers Club that I managed at McGuire Air Force Base in 1996, upon first being introduced to him it was clearly seen that he was in the process of transitioning. Soon after our meeting we became good friends, at that time I considered myself a confessing Christian although I was not living a life that God could get any glory from. I felt a sense of compassion for him being that he was trying so hard to become a woman; I remember feeling extremely sad for him. Here he was an Air Force Officer with a great education and a prospering future and now because of the choices he made, he was now being ostracized and discriminated against. He was also terminated from his employment with one of the major airlines because of his transgender surgery. It was hard to see him as a woman due to his body stature as well as his extremely large bone structure. Despite the surgery he still appeared to be so manly. His mother often praised me for being a close friend of his; she said most people stayed away from him even immediate members of his family. She appreciated our friendship stating that he definitely needed someone he could talk to. Last I heard from him was that he won his lawsuit and was reinstated back to his pilot position for the airline, in addition to teaching college classes on the base.

While serving in the Harvest ministry following Sunday service, I met a young lady at the end of service, the first time she had accepted an invitation to come to Church she welcomed Jesus into her life. At the completion of the service people who made a decision to accept Jesus, join the Church or rededicated their lives were ushered into a room and assigned mentors to walk with them for four (4) weeks to help give clarity to the decisions they had just made. When I came into the room I was introduced to this person by one of the deacons, who then informed me that this was my newly assigned mentee. I was startled to find out that this person was a woman; I thought a mistake was made because she appeared to be a male. At that moment I can recall thinking that here is another one who has been listening to the strange voice and has become confused regarding her gender. I knew then that I had to do what I believed Jesus would do and that was to love her in hopes that one day she would come to the knowledge of who she was created to be, and begin to love herself.

One of my favorite Scriptures can be found in the book of Jerimiah the 29th Chapter, the 11th verse were God says, *"For I know the thoughts and plans that I have for you, says the Lord, thoughts and plans for welfare and peace and not for evil, to give you hope in your final outcome."* I believe that as we move through the journey of our lives God is continually preparing us for things to come. Scripture says, *"Making clear from the first what is to come, and from past times the things which have not so far come about; saying, My purpose is fixed, and I will do all my pleasure" (Isaiah 46:10, BBE).*

At the same Church, again on a Sunday following the service an extremely cute teenage girl came up to me and said, *Deacon Gwen, can I have your phone number I need to talk with you! My response was yes, here is the number and to call me anytime; my husband who was standing next to me spoke to her and said "you better make sure you call her too."*

That same evening the little cute smiley faced teenage girl did exactly what she said and called. I led the conversation in the beginning by asking her how she was doing in school, and then gradually I proceeded to why she needed to speak with me. She surprised me with her transparency as she spurted out "Deacon Gwen, I'm a lesbian!" This kind of took me by surprise, it was definitely something that I didn't expect, and she went on to say that there were at least five (5) of us in the youth ministry at Church. She began to inform me of whom the others were and that she's been unable to control her feelings toward one of the girls who she considered to be her lover. *I recalled as she was speaking that earlier that day when I saw her she had several marks on her neck, looking back they may have been hickies.* I sat on the phone listening to her and waiting for God to instruct me in how to minister to this fourteen (14) year old little girl. Finally God began to speak through me and His compassion for her swelled up on the inside of me for her as well as the other four (4) teenage girls. She began to explain that the others had agreed that they should talk to someone because they knew what they were doing was wrong. She went on to say that I was unanimously nominated to be the one to share this with.

God had been preparing me for this all along, even though I myself could not wrap my understanding around how this could possibly be. These young girls weren't even old enough to walk to the store by themselves let alone carry this heavy burden of having feelings for the same sex and at such an early age. This little innocent looking girl, for now I'll just call her Cutie who was adamant about her state of being, her communication toward me was far above her years. While listening to her talk I began to see her responding to the call of God with such a strong anointing to minister to the other four girls as well as those unknown to her that are secretly living in bondage to this sexual sin. I've come to know that God is perfect and He makes no mistakes and when He calls, He calls in love. He loves everyone no matter who they are, where they have been, or what they have done. He loves each and every person and He died to rescue us all from sin. As His children, we are supposed to love everyone just as He does even though it's much easier sometimes said than done.

For many years I often wondered why God would choose to use me in this area of ministry knowing my life prior to my conversion and the love or need I had for the opposite sex *(today my attraction is only for Pastor Jonathan)*. For years many have opened up to me about their sexual preference, in the same ministry of these little girls and the first encounter I shared earlier in this chapter, another female in her late twenties called me one afternoon and asked to meet with me regarding an issue, she said that she had been trying to deal with this on her own but with no success. I invited her to my home for an early dinner; at this time she openly confessed to me that she had sexual desires for her roommate. This one almost floored me because prior to her revealing this to me someone who I knew who happen to live openly in a lesbian relationship, had made comments jokingly that both she and her roommate were hiding their desires for one another. There were even young men who openly shared with me that they too lived secretly in a homosexual lifestyle. One young man who professed his deliverance from this form of living called to tell me that he was leaving the Church due to another male who was providing him with money and gifts to provoke him back into the lifestyle.

This next incident brought me to tears; I was doing a book signing at a National author's convention. I and Minister Norma were sitting behind my book table and up came this extremely handsome young Caucasian boy. He stood in front of me while browsing through my book *"The Power to Believe,"* he then looked me in the face and said something that brought me to my feet by saying, **"ever since I came out and said that I was gay, my parents and my Church has been very mean to me."** I immediately grabbed this cute little boy and wrapped my arms around him and said in his ear that it's not you that they're angry at; it's the sin of homosexuality. I asked him for his name and age, he replied that his name was Ryan and that he was 16 years old. I then went on and shared with him that sometimes people even family can't handle learning something like this, they have not been prepared to entertain such shocking news especially from their child, and yet so young. I then prayed for him and gave him my number to keep in contact with me. After he walked away I was definitely no longer interested in selling another book.

I too understand how the initial announcement of how this news can be quite a shock to family and friends, if it is unexpected. Chances are the individual giving the announcement have probably been living a life fearful of outright rejection, and even condemnation. It's sad to say that sometimes their worst fears are confirmed by the reactions of those they love. But I honestly can't understand the reaction of his Church unless the Word is not their foundation for ministry. It still amazes me how sins have levels of forgiveness, people put homosexuality way above sins of adultery, fornication, pornography, lying as well as marital abuse. It is time for the Church and its members to understand that sin is definitely sin and it is not limited to the type of sin. Years ago the media didn't do homosexuality any favors, the ugly, lonely, secretly in the closet lifestyle of this sin was never shown, and the way they were portrayed was ridiculous and reduced to a punch line. Today the media promotes it on the wide screen as being a welcomed normal lifestyle with the attempt to redefine marriage. The media has the ability to influence the decision of teens as well as adults when it comes to choosing homosexuality as a lifestyle. We need to and must look at the dangers from the results of promiscuity, which in a spiritual sense it could possibly lead to their demise. That is why our families, churches, as well as our society should offer strong and stable family models. If traditional God ordained marriages and families continue to deteriorate, there is no doubt that both will be redefined forever. The body of believers must not only defend heterosexual marriage, but we need to do a better job of promoting it ourselves.

One of the greatest thing hindering the church from taking a stand against the legitimization of the homosexual lifestyle is its loss of any sort of moral authority. Years back the church set itself apart from the world because it followed and taught the Word of God, but now, however, there is very little difference between the lifestyles and moral practices of the church and those of secular society. The Ecclesia (the church) was called to be pure and holy, set apart, in the world but not of it. It is high time for the born-again believers to live lifestyles consistent with the Word of God. It's time to stop cursing, cheating, lusting, engaging in all sorts of extra-marital sexual activity and submit yourselves to God. The seasons of playing church has to come to an end and it begins with you. We must know and understand that our churches are filled with homosexuals, they are there because they are seeking answers so before you judge, do what God says and study to show yourselves approved. Our job is not to make homosexuals straight, our job is to preach the gospel and make disciples of all nations. The greatest thing that the Body of Christ could possibly do for homosexuals is to bring them to the saving knowledge of Jesus Christ. Yes, homosexuality is a sin like all the others that attach itself to you, but if you're reading this book you already know that Christ died for sinners. His grace and His power are transforming; they leave no willing life unchanged, so let's allow the Holy Spirit to do His work. Seek God's guidance in how to handle the onslaught of this diabolical spirit. Help them to know the truth so they may be set free! Only until we as children of

God begin to live as God would have us live, then we will be able to reach out to the homosexual community in love. Our churches have to become places of refuge for the lost and hurting and our homes should become a place of healing. As the old gospel hymn says, our lives need to become living testimonies of the love and the power of our Creator Elohim.

Our churches have to become places of refuge for the lost and hurting and our homes should become a place of healing. As the old gospel hymn says, our lives need to become living testimonies of the love and the power of our Creator Elohim.

Real ministry is when you can knock the walls
down of your church and confront the spirits
that have so many in our communities bound!

"Who hath saved us, and called us with an holy calling, not according to our works, but according to his own purpose and grace, which was given us in Christ Jesus before the world began"

(2 Timothy 1:9)

CHAPTER 6

Seeing the Evidence

There's one sure-fire way to know what your crop looks like, often we are blinded by what we want to see and actually miss what is seen. My question to you is do you have an accountability partner? Remember, Christlikeness is the state or condition of being Christ like, only others know for sure. The Bible says, *"As the Spirit of the Lord works within us, we become more and more like him, in turn reflecting His glory,"* (2 Corinthians 3:18). The process of changing us to be more like Jesus is called sanctification. We certainly cannot reproduce the character of Jesus in our own strength. Only the Holy Spirit has the power to make the changes God wants to make in our lives. Christlikeness is not produced by imitation, but by inhabitation. *"But what happens when we live God's way? He brings gifts into our lives, much the same way that fruit appears in an orchard—things like affection for others, exuberance about life, and serenity despite condition. We develop a willingness to stick with things, a sense of compassion in the heart, and a conviction that a basic sense of holiness permeates things and people. We find ourselves involved in loyal commitments, not needing to force our way in life, able to marshal and direct our energies wisely"* (Galatians 5:22-23, MSG). We must allow Christ to live in and through us and in some cases we may find a need to have a fruit inspector! Minister Norma is my fruit inspector and I am hers, and I definitely can't forget my husband.

On another note I believe that it's time for the Church to address the issue of *"What to & What Not to Wear!"* Now I'm not saying that mini skirts or dresses, showing all your cleavage or the fact that those skinny jeans are exactly what it says *Skinny Jeans* (or not allowing any distance between your clothing and your skin will affect your salvation). **But if salvation is at work in you it will definitely affect the garments that you choose to clothe your body with. Remember we are new creations and old things should be passed away,** (2 Corinthians 5:17).

This subject has been real important to me in my position as overseer of a women's ministry which is entitled, **"Women Walking in the Spirit."** I have had to address in the members Bylaws modesty in your garments! I have had to address the drinking of wine and other alcoholic beverages, living with a man you are not married to, as well as dealing with an adverse spirit, and I could go on but I'm pretty sure you get the point. All of the women I have had to sit down from serving in the ministry (Women Walking in the Spirit) have been serving in some capacity in their Church for several years. That's why it is of the upmost importance to have an accountability partner who is not afraid to speak truth to power concerning your appearance as well as your character.

A few years ago I had the honor of ministering the gospel to a few hundred women and young girls, some of the women present were women of the street which was visibly apparent by the way they were dressed. The Pastor who sponsored this *OUTSTANDING* event was also involved in prostitution prior to coming to know the Lord Jesus Christ as her personal Savior. These awesome women boldly shared their stories about what led them to the street. Some were dressed very provocative! I have even seen some of the women that confess Christ who wore similar looking garments in the house of the Lord. These women prior to receiving Jesus on the day of this event had no clue of the love between a daughter and her Heavenly Father that's why it is so important for us to be His witness.

Women of God; most of us come to Church every week, some twice a week in my Church and in many others around the world, the Word is strong and sharper than any two-edged sword. Many years ago prior to my conversion the choices I made in what garments I wore was very unbecoming. Upon receiving my salvation as I sat in Church Sunday after Sunday the Word started getting on the inside of me, and soon after that, what was taking place on the inside began to show up on the outside. In other words, salvation got into my Soul! For years I heard ministers teach on the disobedience of Queen Vashti in her denial to come before the king at his request. My mentor Rev. Dr. Eve Lynne Fenton did an awesome teaching in our mentoring training that helped me to understand what actually happened in the Scripture to cause Vashti to lose her position as King Ahasuerus's wife and the title of Queen. What happen was she was a queen in a society that prized modesty in a woman above all else. And at the command of her husband to parade before the drunken crowd, she refused. Far from the action of a rebellious woman, this was the action of a regal queen, refusing to display at the risk of embarrassment and shame. So, she didn't lose her queen ship because of being downright disobedient, she lost it because of her conviction to uphold her moral and modest standard. On the other hand when Queen Esther needed to get an audience with the king without being summons in order to save her people went before the King of kings and her reward was half of everything that king Ahasuerus owned. I truly believe that while in the presence of a Holy God she was endued with His glory, His splendor, His virtue and His grace. No way was the king able to deny her radiance! I also believe that the glory on a woman works on the inside out, showing up in the garments you wear. God is good, He has to be our inside Companion, Hallelujah! With such an inside partner, nothing can stop you! A successful life in the Spirit is no fantasy land; and our salvation is no "pie in the sky by and by" it is a life that we will continually work out, *"Wherefore, my beloved, as ye have always obeyed, not as in presence only, but now much more in my absence, work out your own salvation with fear and trembling. For it is God which worketh in you both to will and to do of his good pleasure"* (Philippians 2:12-13). God the Spirit lives in you in such a tight relationship that everything He promises is within your reach. Hallelujah!

Modesty is of the upmost importance for the women of God, as witnesses unto Christ we must maintain ourselves morally as well, you never know whose watching or admiring us. Our young sisters are very impressionable and whether you know it or not they are watching you and me, in and out of the Church building. I don't want my Pastor or my husband, brothers in Christ and those coming to receive Jesus for the first time to be distracted by your breast or your butt; it is time to cover up. From this point on let's stop dressing like the world, they don't know our Holy God until we introduce them, not only by what we say, but also by what we choose to clothe our bodies, daughters of the Most High let's purpose to dress for the **KING of kings! JESUS CHRIST.**

God has called us to live a separated life in order to avoid the contagion of this corrupt world. Even under the best circumstances and surroundings, Scripture says that fallen man's *"heart is deceitful above all things and desperately wicked";* that his defilement is from within himself also; that there is no hope of redemption and holiness apart from God. The Word of God says as well that *"Ye shall be holy for I Jehovah your God am holy."* We are called to be God's treasure and the instrument of His holy purpose which should be our destiny. For we are, *"a chosen generation, a royal priesthood, a holy nation, a peculiar people; that ye should shew forth the excellencies of him who hath called you out of darkness into his marvelous light"* (1 Peter 2:9). To such separateness, we have been elected.

When I look back over my life and think about the way I use to dress, it makes my stomach nauseous. I thought back in the day that I was most attractive in the least material I used to cover my body. Little did I know that rather than looking attractive, my lack of clothing closely resembled a woman of the street. Our bodies are to be presented as a living sacrifice, holy to God and acceptable (Romans 12:1, 2). This occurs when we come to a saving knowledge of what Christ has done on the cross; in turn He has empowered us through sanctification. By means of the Holy Spirit, who is the Spirit of holiness and power makes our bodies the temple of His presence, producing the fruit of the Spirit. Apostle Paul speaks of this in Galatians 5:22- 23, *"But the fruit of the Spirit is love, joy, peace, patience, kindness, goodness, faithfulness, gentleness and self-control. Against such things there is no law."*

In the Old Testament sanctification was not only with regard to our position in God, but also in regard to life and practice. Again and again through the Word of God we are encouraged to submit ourselves to the sanctity of the Holy Spirit, which is life. Contrasting our former mode of life, Paul addressed the Corinthians: *"Such were some of you: but ye are washed, but ye are sanctified in the name of the Lord Jesus, and by the Spirit of God"* (1 Cor. 6:11). It says that our new man is created in righteousness and true holiness. We are therefore Christ's workmanship created in Him unto good works in which we are to walk, and talk. The Bible says that only the pure in heart shall see God. It is the glorious destiny of the Church (***you are the Church***) to be presented holy and spotless before His glory. Have you ever considered what glory consist of? It is in *"not having spot, or wrinkle, or* *any such thing; but that it should be holy and without blemish,"* (Ephesians 5:26, 27). Every man that has this hope in him purifieth himself, even as he is pure, (1 John 3:3). ***Think on these things as you prepare to get dressed!***

My Fruit Inspector & Best Friend
Minister Norma Gonzalez

My Mentor
Rev. Dr. Eve Lynne Fenton

"Let us walk properly as in the daytime, not in orgies and drunkenness, not in sexual immorality and sensuality, not in quarreling and jealousy. But put on the Lord Jesus Christ, and make no provision for the flesh, to gratify its desire."

(Romans 13:13-14, ESV)

CHAPTER 7

"There Must be No Premarital Impurity"

God has given us clear instruction that all physical love is to be saved for marriage. There are great rewards when this instruction is honored and severe consequences when it is violated. When moral standards are lowered before marriage in order to engage in improper touching or physical intercourse, self-respect is destroyed, communication is damaged, marriage oneness is defiled, fellowship with God is diminished, and physical health is decreased by means of sickness or even death, *"But every man is tempted, when he is drawn away of his own lust, and enticed. Then when lust hath conceived, it bringeth forth sin: and sin, when it is finished, bringeth forth death"* (James 1:14-15). There is no question that immorality can be *pleasurable*: *"Stolen waters are sweet, and bread eaten in secret is pleasant"* (Proverbs 9:17). For this reason Apostle Paul warns us to flee youthful lusts, *"Run away from infantile indulgence. Run after mature righteousness—faith, love, peace—joining those who are in honest and serious prayer before God. Refuse to get involved in inane discussions; they always end up in fights. God's servant must not be argumentative, but a gentle listener and a teacher who keeps cool, working firmly but patiently with those who refuse to obey. You never know how or when God might sober them up with a change of heart and a turning to the truth, enabling them to escape the Devil's trap, where they are caught and held captive, forced to run his errands"* (II Timothy 2:22, MSG). I wish I would have had the knowledge of morality verse immorality when I first engaged in pre-marital sex. I just didn't know the significance of saving yourself until marriage, I didn't know the damage as well as the power that it was capable of having in my future. Growing up in my teenage years my parents never talked about it especially to me, my focus was definitely not on boys all I had on my mind was what I was going to eat next.

When I was twenty-one my oldest sister got pregnant when she was twenty-four years old out of wedlock, (*that's what they called it back then*). Following my mother's discovery of the pregnancy she immediately decided that it would be a good idea for me to be introduced to a birth controlled method. Believe me when I say that at that time I did not have sex nowhere on my mind, I was ashamed to look at my own body let alone allow some young man to see it. Soon after my introduction to birth control a homosexual friend who was very close to me introduced me to appetite suppressants that helped me lose an extremely drastic amount of weight in such a short time. Discovering that I had a brick house underneath all that fat brought about a new attitude along with a desire to exhibit it, my mother began calling me an exhibitionist following the weight lost. With the new body came attraction from the opposite sex that in my previous years never even gave me a mere glance. This is one of the reasons that I stress the importance of having a mentor in your life, at times like these you need someone with wisdom and a leash in order to pull you back when you begin to step out there too far. Once you're out there with no supervision or support it becomes very difficult for you to come back on your own.

When I think back to the un-godly relationships I held on to, it took many years later for me to come to the knowledge that these relationships were not based on love, they were based on my inability to know who I was called to be. Those relationships were only doing what they felt they were created to do and that was to divide and conquer. At that season of my life I was walking according to my own emotions and intellect. God, in His sovereignty knew fully well that my desire was only to satisfy my flesh. Praise the Lord! His Word came into my life to separate my emotions and rationale from my spirit in turn strengthening my faith. We cannot afford to be emotionally driven or so bound by logic that we become spiritually desensitized and unable to walk by faith: after all, *"without faith it is impossible to please God"* (Hebrews 11:6). Today I can say that through Jesus, *"I once was lost but now I am found,"* because God has reconciled us to Himself. Now that He has revived my spirit by placing His Spirit on the inside of me, I can now operate in a spiritual dimension.

I thank God that the Holy Spirit became my mentor, back then I didn't hear a lot about mentorship, or how important it was for me to have an accountability partner in my life. Because of this I found myself living a life with little to no integrity and definitely lacking good character. This became my motivation for dating other women's husbands and without any deep regret or guilt for the wrong that I knew I was committing; neither was I concerned about getting caught. After many seasons of promiscuity I was led by the power of God to live a life of celibacy. Prior to my marriage to Jonathan my first and only husband I had been living a life of celibacy for close to seventeen (17) years. My mind was made up to live a life pleasing not only to God but for my own sanity as well. I purposed to bless God with my body which is the temple of the Holy Spirit. After having several sexual partners in my past, and God sparing me from contracting some form of sexual disease or even death, I purposed to do it God's way by maintaining a lifestyle which includes sustaining from premarital sex *(a born-again virgin is what I called it)*. I truly believe that my past experiences are assisting me in being a strong supportive mentor for the young girls in our mentoring program. I sincerely want to help them skip over the mistakes I made when I was their age. Most of the girls that we mentor are institutionalized or at one time as an adolescence spent a season incarcerated. During our visits to the prison our time is used educating them on the importance of discovering their God given purpose. Some say and truly believe that their previous actions and because of their present residence God is not concern with their present or future well-being. I share with them that through absolute repentance, no talebearer can inform on them, no enemy has the ability to make an accusation stick and forgotten skeleton can't come tumbling out of the closet to abash them by trying to destroy their self-confidence and expose their past. Despite the devil's knowledge of our affliction and the adversities of life which are more than theoretic, whatever may befall us, God alone knows and cares as no one else can.

When I share with them the importance of abstaining from pre-marital sex they somehow believe that it is not possible. In hearing the stories they share in these meetings and the poetry they write helps me and the other women in the ministry understand how girls so young can end up with such a low self-image of themselves and the thought that not even God could ever love them. Most if not all of them have done things in such a short time that has opened the door for life to beat them down to the point of having little to no remorse. They have become so numb to what is good that some believe they are in love with one another while in confinement. Many of the young girls who consider themselves to be homosexual, once released, end up getting pregnant. Some even fall prey to a spirit of prostitution and end up getting involved in sex trafficking, which is a gateway to becoming addicted, to illicit drugs and other unlawful activities. The ministry doesn't go into the institutions in order to whip these girls into shape by exercising our ability to quote a myriad of Scriptures; we go in, in hopes of encouraging them to live healthy as well as holistic lives. Our going is to represent Christ and use our knowledge of God's love in hopes of evoking a positive change in their lives. In addition we want to make them aware of the consequences of sin, should they choose to return to their old lifestyle.

I find it mind boggling that many of them as well as a large number of high school students who have a limited knowledge or in some cases even care about the possibilities of contracting HIV or even AIDS. There have been cases that even after being confined in an institution some end up contracting the virus which is another form of incarceration. I experienced my first encounter with fornication at the age of twenty-one. Some may say that at that age you are considered grown but living with my parents and not paying any rent, and being sexually active didn't equate with being grown. Back then I was introduced to AIDS due to having a close friend who I called my pretend brother who eventually died of AIDS. In addition to being a homosexual he was an intravenous drug user as well. However because he was too busy living his life he never took the time to investigate why his outer appearance was drastically changing. I often say that *"what you don't know will eventually hurt you, or even kill you."*

Statistics show that HIV diagnoses among 13 to 19 year olds, almost 70 percent of them are African Americans, even though they constitute a much smaller proportion of the adolescent population in the U.S. Almost 80 percent of all adolescent infections are to males. Nine out of 10 adolescent male HIV infections result from male-to-male sexual contact. The same proportions of adolescent females are infected from heterosexual contact. Studies show although HIV testing is widely available and no cost to the individual, self-reported rates of HIV testing have remained flat in recent years. Fifty-four percent of high school students have had sex at least once this is over half of its population, yet only 13 percent report ever having had an HIV test.

How often do you find yourself sitting in a pew at Church and hearing an informational message about our teenage girls in this era of HIV/AIDS? Or witness your Pastor, standing at the pulpit, encouraging his congregation to stay informed, while encouraging them to be aware of their daughters' pressures, their school environment, and friends. Teaching them that sexual curiosity does in fact change from generation to generation because of the impact of the media we must provide training for females 'or young adult ministries in order to have that special "smart sex talk" especially in our Churches. I often say *that those who know better do better.* Because the lines of right and wrong have been virtually erased in our culture, those that are trapped by the enemy into sexual sin are encouraged most often to embrace their iniquity rather than feel convicted. The media of course has and is playing a major role in affecting the family view of sexuality; marriage and family life. Positive role models are few and far between and negative examples are both normalized and glorified. Today we see family responsibilities and the consequences of sexual freedom are most often downplayed while sexuality without boundaries is portrayed as ideal and carefree. The more those messages are received and applied to everyday life, the more damage is done to the family. Sex outside of marriage is a near constant theme within today's media, but rarely is the ugly side shown, the side that shows the fatherless homes and the unwanted pregnancies as well as sexually transmitted diseases. Also there is the effect of emotional harm that can result from sleeping with multiple partners. I must put special emphasis on the consequences of this action, which can be devastating. The media has offered many unhealthy ideas to our families and children; you can even see the effects of this within the body of Christ.

The media also has the capability of teaching our young girls and in some cases grown women that they need to weigh around one hundred pounds in order to be considered attractive to the opposite sex. It has also taught our teenage girls the need to sleep with their boyfriends in order to be loved as well as the less clothing they wear the more attractive they become. Single motherhood has been presented as a feminist ideal with very few young girls realizing exactly how hard their lives are going to be because of it. Several of the young girls in our mentoring program who spent a season or seasons of incarceration after their release have found themselves becoming mothers even before they are able to acquire State Drivers Licenses. I personally have been affected through the years with two of my nieces who became pregnant prior to graduating from High School.

The question is how can our society and our families be any greater than the heroes we put before us? In addition to looking at the real-life consequences of the ideas being advocated by the media, we also need to begin portraying good role models through the media. I'd like to encourage and challenge our spiritual leaders to begin to speak out and to use their platform to educate their congregation and those that God has entrusted in their care. If the family of God would join together in hopes of provoking the media to show the benefits of a family staying together, a father who's involved in the lives of his children and couples waiting until marriage before having sex, as well as the amazing power of God to transform lives. In doing this I believe we will then begin to see the deterioration of our marriages and families reversed. If helping to preserve marriage means that Pastors need to preach more about marriage and the importance of faithfulness from the pulpits, then they just better preach it. Even if it means bringing married couples into the schools to talk with our youth about how to have successful marriages, then we have to put things in place to make that happen by getting those school doors opened. Together we should put a demand on our politicians to start introducing legislation that benefits marriage and family and then we have to make sure that we vote for it. I believe and I pray that you do as well, believe that marriage and family is too important to the functioning of our society to simply just sit back and allow it to fall by the wayside. I would like to encourage the readers to live and act according to the Scripture found in Philippians Chapter 4 verse 8, which says, *"Finally brethren, whatever things are true, whatever things are noble, whatever things are just, whatever things are pure, whatever things are lovely, whatever things are of good report, if there is any virtue and if there is anything praiseworthy—meditate on these things."* Because if we are willing and able to apply the values found in the Word to our marriages and families, they will in fact grow strong and will definitely not fail.

I have not always done what is right in the sight of God or behind the backs of my parents and even today sometimes I fall short, but I thank God for the life that I have chosen to live today. I find it to be my duty as well as responsibility to help our young girls discover their purpose and stop allowing their past to dictate how they should live in the present as well as in their future. If they never come to repentance, our Lord Jesus Christ cannot lead them back into the best that He has created for them to experience. It starts with loving yourself enough to search out the plan that God has for you and that's where spiritual mothers and fathers partner to raise up communities of successful young men and women with a love that's eternal. *"A new command I give you: Love one another. As I have loved you, so you must love one another"* (John 13:34, NIV).

"God's Original Plan"
The Wilkins Family!

"So clean house! Make a clean sweep of malice and pretense, envy and hurtful talk. Now, like infants at the breast, drink deep of God's pure kindness. Then you'll grow up mature and whole in God. You've had a taste of God. Welcome to the living Stone, the source of life. The workmen took one look and threw it out; God set it in the place of honor. Present yourselves as building stones for the construction of a sanctuary vibrant with life, in which you'll serve as holy priests offering Christ-approved lives up to God. The Scriptures provide precedent: Look! I'm setting a stone in Zion, a cornerstone in the place of honor. Whoever trusts in this stone as a foundation will never have cause to regret it."

(1 Peter 2:1-6, MSG)

CHAPTER 8

Jesus Knows How to Deliver the Godly Out of Temptation

As you have read thus far you can see how I have used myself as well as other women's experiences to help you get an understanding of the need to change and become the person God has created us to be, so that you can live the life that He has preordained for you and I to live. As I have stated in the first chapter that there has to be a complete surrender, or you can say a total turnaround from the direction that you have been going in order to experience the life to which you have been called. God has given us several biblical characters to help us clearly see His ability to bring us out of temptation and ungodly situations that sometimes we put ourselves in. For example Abrahams nephew Lot, you have probably said to yourself what in the world was a man like Lot doing in a place like Sodom and Gomorrah, and why would Peter use him to illustrate how a man of genuine faith could fall into sin and deception. I don't believe it was because he was ignorant regarding the dangers of sin; he simply ignored and tolerated sin until the sinful environment of Sodom and Gomorrah wore down his resistance. Therefore he made critical judgment errors about himself and his family and laid his morals on the line and it eventually cost him his wife and his children. I know that in the past I had made some pretty poor decisions that could of possibility been detrimental for myself as well as others. If not for the grace and mercies of God I would have not made it to this point in my life. I'm more than pretty sure that someone was interceding for me in the seasons of my ignorance. Evil is all around us in today's society birthed out of deception, we become victims of stealing, lying, drugs, sex trafficking, pornography and violence. God is calling us to be holy and set apart, not to be influenced by this present day culture which is under the dominants of Satan. Sin will always have consequences.

If it had not been for Uncle Abraham, the consequence of Lot's decision would have been death. It was because of his family that Abraham stood yet before the Lord. Abraham knew that if he did not come to Lots rescue he and his family would have been wiped out by one sweep of a hand as the judgment of God fell upon Sodom and Gomorrah. This provoked Uncle Abraham to take on a serious role in an act of intercession before the Lord. Genesis 18:23 says, *"And Abraham drew near, and said, Wilt thou destroy the righteous with the wicked?"* The fact that God could call this kind of prayer communion clearly lets us know that God loves it when His children come to Him to make straightforward demands on behalf of others, *"And the Lord went His way, as soon as He had finished communing with Abraham; and Abraham returned unto his place"* (Genesis 18:33). The Scripture says that after interceding Abraham returned home and continued in his daily rituals knowing that he had ensured the safety of Lot and his family through the power of intercession. He was able to sleep in peace with the confidence that God's hand would honor his righteous, but backslidden nephew who was living in the city of Sodom and Gomorrah. It brings a peace within your soul when you know without a doubt that someone else has been delivered from destruction, and now made safe, because you made the decision to stand in the gap and pray for them. And for this reason alone Abraham was able to return home and go to bed and enjoy sweet sleep. He knew that God would honor His requests and his nephew Lot's life would be preserved. Genesis 19:29 says, *"And it came to pass, when God destroyed the cities of the plain, that God remembered Abraham, and sent Lot out of the midst of the overthrow, when he overthrew the cities in which Lot dwelt."* Lot did the things he did because he chose to live in his old sin nature and do what was easy, and he made choices to flirt with evil instead of living to honor God. As a result of their association Lot and his family including the nation of Israel suffered for years to come. The lesson for us is in making choices that do not conform to the world but to the contrary submitting to the Word of God, which will guide us into living lives that are pleasing to God. If it had been left up to Lot, Lot would have been consumed in the iniquity of the city. He had become callous and ensnared by his surrounding to know that he needed to be delivered. Therefore, it was for Abraham's sake that Lot was delivered. Because of Abraham's act of intercession on behalf of the righteous God delivered Lot from pending destruction.

We must make it our goal to pray for those who we know are caught in sin, people may be so deceived that they are unaware of how critical their situation really is. If left to themselves, they will probably continue on the same course of action, and end up experiencing divine retribution. Ultimately we need to thank God; through interceding we can make a difference on their behalf. By standing in the gap on the behalf of error-ridden individuals, many have been spared and brought back into a place of restoration and usefulness. I know that if it were not for the prayers of the righteous which availeth much and earnestly prayed for me, I too may have stayed in my tailor made sin and not experienced the blessings that I have today.

God always gives us the ability to do things different so that we might enjoy the life that He has planned for us. Scripture says in Romans 12:1-2, *"I beseech you therefore, brethren, by the mercies of God, that ye present your bodies a living sacrifice, holy, acceptable unto God, which is your reasonable service. And be not conformed to this world: but be ye transformed by the renewing of your mind, that ye may prove what is that good, and acceptable, and perfect, will of God.*" God desires for us to genuinely walk in His Agape Love while displaying His wisdom and depending upon His power, not just talking about it, but to be about it as well.

Pray for Others!

"We who have run for our very lives to God have every reason to grab the promised hope with both hands and never let go. It's an unbreakable spiritual lifeline, reaching past all appearances right to the very presence of God where Jesus, running on ahead of us, has taken up his permanent post as high priest for us, in the order of Melchizedek."

(Psalm 110.4)

CHAPTER 9

"Eye of the Storm"

Often I think about all the trials and tribulations that I have endured most were in my early years. Please do not get me wrong, I'm not saying that I don't experience any now because I most certainly do. You see now my outlook on life is so much different because I know that I can take whatever ills me to the altar and walk away knowing that God's got it, and as long as I don't keep picking it up, all I have to do is trust that He alone can work it all out for my good.

Since allowing God to manage my life I now have the affirmation that no matter what comes my way He alone can keep me in the ***"eye of the storm."*** Let me help you understand what I mean when I say the ***"eye of the storm."*** This is a specific spot in the center of a twister, hurricane, or tornado that is calm, this area is isolated from the frantic frenzy of the activity that is purposed to take you out. In the storm you find that everything around the center is violent and turbulent, but the center remains peaceful (that's God). Life is so sweet when all hell is breaking loose around you and you are calm and serene in the midst of chaos, in the ***"eye of your storm."***

Take for instance the eagle; he loves the storms he gets excited when the clouds gather. He uses the storm's wind to lift it higher than he's ever been before far above the clouds. This gives him the opportunity to glide while resting its wings. In the meantime all the other birds are hiding in the leaves and branches of the trees. Like the eagle we should use the storms of life to raise us to greater heights rather than send us away defeated and discouraged.

When You Have a Presence-Consciousness

I recall hearing my Pastor who happens to be my husband share with our congregation when the eagle gets around thirty or forty years old his feathers begin to quiver and dry up and cling to the eagle's body. At this time he makes his way to the highest cleft in the mountains and there he plucks out all his feathers. At this time he also beats his beak against the cleft causing it to fall off, and after five to six months of painful development his beak and feathers grow back adding an additional thirty to forty more years to his life. It's from this perspective that the prophet Isaiah writes, *"But they that wait upon the LORD shall renew their strength; they shall mount up with wings as eagles; they shall run, and not be weary; and they shall walk, and not faint"* (Isaiah 40:31).

If you have read either of my previous books, you would better understand what I'm talking about when I speak of being in the **"eye of the storm."** Even now I find myself every now and then looking back on that particular time in my life whereas in the wee, wee hours of the morning I felt my life slipping away. I recall lying in a pool of blood on the vinyl floor of our basement family room. The floor was cold but the blood running down my backside seemed to feel like hot oil. Though it appeared that hell was breaking loose in my body, I was still able to sense the presence of God. That's why it is so important that we remind ourselves that God is with us, in us, and among us. Our failure to think of Him as not always being with us may result in being displeasing in the sight of God. He is just as with you in spirit as He would be in the flesh. When we have a presence-consciousness *(which is the title of my fourth book)* it allows us to experience the anointing that accompanies His presence. Therefore, we must make it a habit of practicing His presence. Even though it looked like the enemy was winning I could rest in the assurance that God was moving mightily on my behalf. Once you have made the transition and have relinquished control to God, He can help you master life situations that may confront you from time to time. By making this a practice, pretty soon you'll learn how to live in the **"eye of the storm."**

Gwendolyn Ann Cook

"Only as high as I reach can I grow, only as far as I seek can I go, only as deep as I look can I see, only as much as I dream can I be."

-Karen Ravn

Soaring Eagle!

"Keep vigilant watch over your heart; that's where life starts. Don't talk out of both sides of your mouth; avoid careless banter, white lies, and gossip. Keep your eyes straight ahead; ignore all sideshow distractions. Watch your step, and the road will stretch out smooth before you. Look neither right nor left; leave evil in the dust."

(Proverbs 4:25-27)

CHAPTER 10

Look Straight Ahead

When considering the instructions given in this Scripture I began pondering over it and came to the realization that so often in my past, I found it extremely hard to keep looking straight ahead. I was often fearful of my future, not that the sickness was going to kill me because one thing for sure I was not afraid of dying, I knew that Heaven was my destination. So often during seasons of sickness and disease it appeared that I was so close to death that I could smell the devils breathe. The fear came from not being sure of what my future had in store for me; the pain I continually experienced interfered with my ability to see into the future. Many of my young adult years were spent in and out of the hospital dealing with one attack of sickness after the other.

In discovering this particular Scripture which is filled with many promises that could be mine if I hearkened to them, by avoiding the distractions that life in this world sometimes bring. The instructions here informed me to watch my step, and the end result was that the road would stretch out smooth before me. It continues by saying look neither to the right nor to the left; leave evil in the dust. In order to do this I had to stay true to my confession of being a *"Born Again Believer."*

No Time for Distractions!

On another note I have witnessed many who confess Christ but live a life so conforming to the world that it's hard to tell that they are *"Born Again Believers."* I believe! (*my opinion only*) that their lifestyle resembles that of the world, plus their testimony of living for the Lord is so off the path of righteousness that it could possibly cause others to stumble. In the newness of my new created life I allowed those who I thought where doing it right, with the knowledge that they had been in the Church for a long time, yet still partying, drinking and even fornicating. At the time I called myself following God, but ultimately following them, even though their witness was apparently pretty shaky.

I also believe that one of the reasons for mine, and possibly your setbacks in various seasons of our lives was that we allowed many distractions to seduce us into losing our focus. I was too busy looking at people instead of looking at God, I found myself following them straight to hell. Because of this I often found myself outside of my purpose, opening the door for our adversary to have a voice in my ear. I can recall tripping so many times that I didn't even know who I was; I had forgotten who God had said I was and turned my focus on becoming something that I wasn't in order to please everyone else except Him. Because of the lessons learned I came to know that the biggest battles in your life were in the realm of your soul, your mind, your emotions and your will, because that's where the devil operates. If he can get your mind off the Word and have your emotions running wild, then your will can and will most often swing toward sin. The key in the soulish realm is to stay focused on the Word of God; then you can be led by the Spirit of God, *"I've told you this so that my peace will be with you. In the world you'll have trouble. But cheer up! I have overcome the world"* (John 16:33).

In verse 26 of Proverbs Chapter 4 the word "ponder" means to think about the path you are launching out on. It says make sure you are heading out on that which leads to righteousness, don't despair on the path that you have chosen. Keep your path straight and do not allow the world and what it can possibly offer you or people to attract you off of it. I think this is so profound, and even today I continue to thank God for the revelation of this Scripture. This particular Scripture also helped me to discern other people especially when it comes to how they look at you; I have discovered that eyes are like a window which gives you the ability to look into ones soul. Take shifty eyes for an example, people with shifty eyes cannot look you straight on when they are talking to you, which is an indication that they have something they are covering up. Eyes that can look you straight on say, "I am telling the truth." And I don't even want to go into what wandering eyes can mean that's totally another book.

Many times after my conversion the enemy would use the opposite sex as a diversion to provoke me off of my preordained path. I believe the enemy knows your unsaved past only because at that time in your life he was your employer. In an attempt to set you back he will often create situations that could possibly sabotage your success in living your life as a new creature in Christ. Jesus declared that His Word was to bring us peace in the midst of the storm and when your world seems to be turned upside down, His Word will comfort you, give you wisdom, and inspire you to do the brave and courageous thing. Take this for instance if a married woman looks across the room and sees a good looking man, and her flesh rises up with a desire for him and says, *"Lord have mercy, isn't he fine,"* it's then time for her to rule her body and get her mind on God's Word. And by the power of the Holy Spirit inside of you command your flesh to yield to the Word of God, *"But I keep under my body, and bring it into subjection: lest that by any means, when I have preached to others, I myself should be a castaway* (1 Corinthians 9:27). That is why when temptation knocks at your door, you must say yes to the Word of God; then you will have the inner fortitude to say no to your flesh. I know that I have stated this throughout the book and please pardon me if I continue to be redundant, but again I say that mentorship is of the upmost importance as well as an accountability partner. I don't even have to ask Dr. Eve my mentor what she would think or say if I started hanging out with the women from the "Housewives of Atlanta or the L.A. Preachers Wives" on reality television. All I know is she would sit me down and minister to me the possible outcome of these new found friends. The devil knows exactly how to distract you and seduce you out of your God ordained purpose. We can look at James 1:14-15 where it says, *"But every man is tempted, when he is drawn away of his own lust, and enticed. Then when lust hath conceived, it bringeth forth sin: and sin, when it is finished, bringeth forth death."*

*"Wherefore - Because I remember this, I remind thee of stirring up -
Literally, blowing up the coals into a flame.
The gift of God - has given thee."*

(2 Timothy 1:6)

CHAPTER 11

Digging Up Your Dormant Gifts

Have you ever just knew you were called to a thing, a ministry or even an office and the people that you were submitted up under, year after year insisted on telling you that that's wasn't God? Well then this is the chapter for you!

I had been serving in a ministry for several years, this particular Church offered several areas of ministries you could possibly serve in. I first began serving in the two (2) ministries that were closes to my heart, and I believe God's heart as well, *prayer & evangelism*. I strongly believe that prayer and evangelism go hand in hand in order to be effective in any ministry. I had grown to be very passionate about the both of them and devoted my life to being a woman of prayer with a desire to see everyone I encountered receive salvation.

I definitely didn't expect to get involved in ministry without the preparation needed; I recall the Pastor often saying that the indication that you have a calling is your desire to prepare for it. That's why I made it a point to study the Word of God, Scripture says in 2 Timothy 2:15 *"And take care of yourself, that you present yourself perfectly before God, a laborer without shame, who preaches the word of truth straightforwardly."* The verse here illustrates the need for me to understand that word meanings may change, and being one who is called to a ministry or an office must be ever on guard against misapplying or twisting Scripture, even when we purpose on preaching the truth. Understanding the meaning to strive or be diligent in handling accurately the Word of truth was my aim. When you choose to keep your mind on God's Word, you are then operating in the language of your spirit and the Holy Spirit. By doing it this way you are then subjecting your soul to your spirit, and you have the motivation and the strength to keep yourself in line. Staying focus on what God says, you are allowing the Holy Spirit to rule you through your spirit. This is how you manifest the kingdom of God in your life. But on the other hand when you focus on worldly thoughts and worldly thinking you are operating in the devil's language and that is subjecting your soul to your flesh which allows Satan to rule you through your senses and your own self-centered thinking manifesting the devil's kingdom in your life.

While taking a course in Hermeneutics I discovered how I myself and many others often used Scripture out of content. My goal was to become an approved workman by living a life faithfully before God and sometimes even to the point of suffering. I'm not speaking here of suffering like that of a martyr, but one who continued in the path of righteousness even in the face of adversity even if it came from those I was called to serve.

God Will Resist You until You Submit To Authority

Can I tell you that something strange happens to the mind when it tastes authority and power, especially when the taste of authority and power comes too quickly. I have witnessed people get promoted and elevated into lofty positions of authority quickly and it opened a door for the devil to come in and create a false delusion of spiritual grandeur for them. I certainly did not want to become like some others I knew in the church that had been quickly inducted into the leadership and became so impressed by his or her spiritual advancement that they began to think they are something very "extra." There is something about it that cannot bear the light of the Word of God. We have to live and serve in the order and the authority of God, and see that everything is bearing you on to greater heights and depths and a greater knowledge of the love of God. This is the very reason that I believe Apostle Paul commanded Timothy, *"Not a novice, lest being lifted up with pride he fall into the condemnation of the devil"* (1 Timothy 3:6, KJV). Paul is clearly warning us that if one is elevated too quickly into a place of notoriety in the ministry, you are placing this person in a position to be tempted in the same way that Lucifer was tempted. I was faithful in the natural things that I was called to do, even when I didn't care to do some of what I was assigned to. I had understood that until you can identify with the one that has authority over you that you are serving, you are not ready to be in a position of authority yourself. First Peter 5:5-6 says, *"Likewise, ye younger, submit yourselves unto the elder. Yea, all of you be subject one to another, and be clothed with humility: for God resisteth the proud, and giveth grace to the humble. Humble yourselves therefore under the mighty hand of God, that he may exalt you in due time."* God will resist you until you submit to authority. He put you under the person you are serving, to serve them as unto the Lord. So I honored the Pastors, Elders and Ministers, and the G-12 Leader whom God set me under. I found pleasure in serving, even the ones who obviously did not like me. I recall being in my prayer closet one day praying for some of the leaders of the Church who often responded negatively to anything I would say or do. Soon after I came out of my prayer time my mother who was probably listening began to share with me. She went on to say, *that jealousy is a spirit and its big in the Church, she said that you are definitely a Christian because how can you stay at that Church doing what you do and it goes unappreciated. She said, that's not the only Church around here, you need to go back into your prayer room and ask God to send you to another Church.* I began to share with her that I cannot leave until God tells me to, and I have yet to hear Him say anything about me moving on.

In knowing my calling regardless of what I had to come up against, and sometimes it was often other Christians I stayed faithful to the ministry. Luke 16:12 says, *"And if ye have not been faithful in that which is another man's, who shall give you that which is your own?"* I knew that being faithful with what belongs to somebody else, God will give you your own. If you're not faithful in taking care of others stuff, ministry or visions God isn't going to give you your own. That's why I have served everyone I have worked for or served under faithfully to help him or her fulfill their purpose. I was faithful in that Church and when I left after several years of some good training, I didn't leave with a murmuring spirit. I left knowing that God had equipped me there to release me to where I'm at, and yet still journeying, *"For the perfecting of the saints, for the work of the ministry, for the edifying of the body of Christ: Till we all come in the unity of the faith, and of the knowledge of the Son of God, unto a perfect man, unto the measure of the stature of the fullness of Christ:"* (Ephesians 4:12-13). For that purpose I dedicated my God given gifts including my natural talents to the ministry, and God has stayed faithful to His Word.

Waiting on God!

All of the gifts that I had received from the teaching and training through my willingness and obedience in that ministry, God today is using them; including the new gifts He has endowed me with for the ministry that He has so graciously given me. My advice to you is to continue in your walk of obedience and stay faithful where you serve, God has given us all gifts, *"But having different gifts, according to the grace which has been given to us, whether [it be] prophecy, [let us prophesy] according to the proportion of faith;* (Romans 12:6, DBT). Wait on God, and those gifts that you have allowed to stay dormant for so long, He will tell you and assist you when the time comes to put them to use for His glory and for His purpose. I left that ministry knowing that God had called me out and He was going to use me as an agent in His army.

One thing that has often left me confused is when you respond to God's calling and leave a ministry after you have given yourself, gifts and talents for well over a decade, and you are led by the Spirit of God to do so, you are in some cases ostracized and treated as a cast away. At one time was considered a leader in that ministry yet after leaving I felt then as well as today that I could never go back even for a visit. Being a member of a family should not change no matter where you choose to live *(The Family of God)*. You like me may be confronted with situations like this, but don't allow it to discourage you. Sometimes when you are called out of a ministry, even though the leadership may not respond to your departure the way you would have hoped, possibly the reason they take on a less than godly attitude toward you is that they may feel as though you are leaving them, and take you're leaving very personal. Stay in prayer and God will eventually mend their hearts, I'm praying that one day the ministry that I was called out of would recall all the good I had done to be a blessing and one day soon welcome me back with the understanding that my season there had eventually come to an end.

Trillis Irene Greene
Mom
June 14, 1935 – December 4, 2012

"And I am convinced and sure of this very thing, that He Who began a good work in you will continue until the day of Jesus Christ [right up to the time of His return], developing [that good work] and perfecting and bringing it to full completion in you."

(Philippians 1:6)

CHAPTER 12

He's Not Finished With Me Yet!

One thing for sure is that as you grow in your relationship with God your relationship with people will change. Even in the Church! When you achieve some success believe me, it will test all of your relationships because some may become insecure or even fade away, but this will help you to identify whether that relationship was spiritual or fleshly. When I began to grow in the things of God I discovered who at the time had recognized the hand of God on my life or who was actually just sitting around playing church, therefore, my success was putting them under conviction and they were not happy with the change, nor were they excited about the elevation that was taking place in my life. I began to realize that those who have continuously said they loved me were actually with me only because of convenience. Convenient love, loves somebody for what you can get out of them. You must make sure that you come to know people after the spirit, not the flesh. You must also be careful that folks don't love your flesh because that is considered flattery, not honor. I have discerned that some of my past relationships were like that; therefore they needed to be exposed and now they are no longer a part of my life. When you can recognize someone whom God is blessing, you are recognizing God, and when you honor a vessel God is using, you too are honoring the Lord.

My dear sisters this is the season as well as the time of the awakening for the women of God, a time for you to be very sensitive to the things that may influence you. Jealousy, envy, backbiting, gossiping and a cantankerous attitude has to come to an end. It is time for you to wake up to God's plan and purpose for your life. He is about to raise up women in an incredible way, timing is extremely important as well as your character. I, like most women can be impatient and want to know something before it's time, expecting a microwave move of God in our lives. That's why we have to be patient and wait as well as watch for Him to move, while we are preparing to enter at the proper time so that we can see His glory revealed.

Understand Your Invaluable Worth

Today, we must inquire of God and seek to find out how He desires to raise us up to influence His kingdom and the world. We must also recognize how Satan's plans depend on the continued oppression of the women of God. You can clearly see if you have been walking with God for a while that women happen to be the most untapped resource. I believe, and I hope you believe, ***"that there's never been a better time in history to be a girl than it is right now."*** N o w is the time my sisters, for you to understand your invaluable worth and get into the alignment that God has for you so that you can exercise the unique gifts and calling that the Lord has for you in this season. Our destiny is linked with our expectations. Therefore, we must be whole in our emotions if we are going to embrace what God wants to do with us, our desires must be in position and in alignment with His desires for us. ***Just because you have been demonized in your past does not mean that you can't outwit the devil today!*** You cannot move to your future by living in your past. The Lord is calling people like you and me in this hour, through the power of prayer where we can gain the wisdom that will surely dethrone the thrones of iniquity where they have been able to be established. The basis for strategic prayer that outwits our enemy comes from our understanding of our position with God. As believers we are in a covenant relationship with God, and everything we have and everything we are will flow from this covenant relationship. We can't be afraid to confront those things that would hinder spiritual breakthrough and deliverance for ourselves, families, friends and ministries.

As you read and meditate in the Word of God you can discover how God has used His daughters to assist Him in times past. In this season I honestly believe that we, meaning women are enjoying more opportunities than ever to become all that God has created us to be, therefore it is time to dig up all of those buried gifts and allow our lights to shine all for the glory and purposes of God. It's time for women who have been prepared as well as disciplined with faith and with a holy boldness to confront and overthrow that which is bent on the destruction of the family, the church and our nation. Girl! In this season if you have been experiencing feelings of being totally abandoned, you must know that the Lord can raise you up and prepare you for when He will use you, for the advancing of His kingdom. There are women reading this book right now that have been faithful to their church, but have not been faithful nor have they been committed to the call of God on their lives. Many have allowed their gifts to lay dormant for so long that some even have forgotten that they are still operable.

The Importance of Timing!

Today we can see a fresh generations of Esther's, Deborah's, Sarah's, and wise women like the woman found in 2 Samuel 20:16-17, where it says, *"Then a wise woman cried out from the city, "Hear, Hear! Please say to Joab, 'Come nearby, that I may speak with you.'" When he had come near to her, the woman said, "Are you Joab?" He answered, "I am." Then she said to him, "Hear the words of your maidservants." And he answered, "I am listening."* A discreet woman, by her prudent management, satisfied Joab, and yet saved the city. Jesus chose a woman to be the person to whom He first appeared, and she became the prototype of the believer spreading the good news of salvation to the world. In the book of Genesis the 24th Chapter reveals a different dimension regarding women that God wants us to understand in this season. It talks about Isaac who was given Abrahams heritage, however he couldn't perpetuate the inheritance by himself. So Abraham sent his servant to find a suitable bride for Isaac. When Abraham's servant arrived in Mesopotamia in the evening, he made his camels kneel down outside the city of Nahor by a well of water. The time of the day was extremely important because the evening was the time when the women of the city would come out to draw water. Scripture says, *"Behold, I am standing by the spring of water, and the daughters of the men of the city are coming out to draw water. Let the young woman to whom I shall say, 'Please let down your jar that I may drink,' and who shall say, 'Drink, and I will water your camels'—let her be the one whom you have appointed for your servant Isaac. By this[a] I shall know that you have shown steadfast love to my master."* Abraham's servant was looking and listening carefully for a woman to fulfill God's prophetic command at that time. And when she said the right thing, he knew she was the one. There is a perfect timing for everything, and this is a time that men and women must position themselves properly. I can go on and on talking to you about how God has used women in times past and the fact that He desires to use you today as well. Wisdom is not confined to rank or sex; it consists not in deep knowledge; but in understanding how to act as matters arise, that troubles may be turned away and benefits secured. Do you now understand what this means for us? When you do that which God is asking you to do in His perfect timing, then one way or another you will receive your blessing.

God Opens Doors!

I am still in awe of the doors that God has opened for me as well as the doors that He has closed. It still amazes me when I think about how I was used for a season in hosting my own broadcast on ION Television as well as an opportunity to run a sixty second commercial promoting my first book *"The Power To Believe."* That open door gave me the freedom to speak truth to power and to tell the world that there's power in believing God's Word. Also in the following season I was asked to host one of the nation's largest Christian networks when I was afforded the opportunity to be one of the hosts for the Trinity Broadcast Network (TBN). God truly blessed me, as the host I was considered a volunteer meaning with no pay, but on the other hand they hired my husband as my camera man. It was totally an awesome experience to have Jonathan filming me as I interviewed men and women of God, many who I handpicked to be on the broadcast. I recall receiving a letter from the founder and owner Brother Paul Crouch for the first time addressing me as Evangelist Gwendolyn Ann Cook, and in the letter he was sharing with me the direction that the network was moving in. I was extremely grateful for the opportunity to be a part of the TBN family, but it was hard to understand that the majority of those employed at the Pennsylvania studio did not have a relationship with Jesus. Matter of fact the station manager said to me often that she didn't believe in Church, and that she used Barns and Noble to study the Word of God on her own.

Another door opened while sitting in the family room of our home with my husband one evening and receiving a call inviting me with an opportunity to represent the State of New Jersey as the National Organizer for the annual "White House Prayer Initiative." The Founder Rev. Terry Lee was preparing to celebrate the fourteenth year of mobilizing churches to gather in our Nation's Capital, Washington, D.C. on the first Saturday following the National Day of Prayer to pray for our President, his family and all the other Leaders of our nation on the Southside of the White House Lawn. Through my acceptance of the invitation I was invited to travel to Brooklyn, New York for a Prayer Breakfast for this initiative. The Keynote Speaker for the breakfast was Presidential Appointee Dr. Jannah Scott who sits in the office of Deputy Director at the DHS Center for Faith-based and Neighborhood Partnerships a Department of the White House. I knew then that this too was an open door from God, with the city of Camden, N.J. earning the title of having the highest crime ranking in the nation as well as being named the poorest city in America I saw this as an opportunity to seek some federal help. I purposed to get an audience with a White House representative in hopes of obtaining some assistance for the city of Camden and its residents.

As a result of the compassion and love I have for the city I was compelled to share with Dr. Jannah the plight of the city and requested that she would look into what could possibly be done on the federal government level to help prevent youth gang, gun violence, open air drug distribution, prostitution and other criminal activity. And just maybe this could bring employment opportunities back into the city. Through this encounter I was able to invite Dr. Jannah to Camden so that she could meet and have some dialogue with Camden's Mayor

Dana Redd, and Chief John Scott Thomson of the Camden Police Department. I also invited over one hundred Pastors in the city as well; unfortunately, only about seven (7) showed up. Although the majority of the faith community chose not to attend this forum I in turn became their representative. I too pray that, ***"When I stand before God at the end of my life, I would hope that I would not have a single bit of talent left, and could say I used everything you gave me!" –Erma Bombeck***

God moved on Camden's behalf, in that same year, the US Department of Justice selected Camden City to receive a National Forum on Youth Violence Prevention expansion project planning grant. Even up until this present day Camden is reaping the financial benefits from that meeting. Today businesses are coming into the city bringing jobs for the residents, the NBA 76ers have found a way to be a blessing to Camden by hosting the inaugural Camden Youth Basketball Clinic. Also the 76ers will bring their new Training Complex to Camden following the construction of their new facility. Amongst several other grants, Camden has been named a Federal Promise Zone being one out of eight cities across America designated as a "promise zone" by President Obama's Administration. The designation will give Camden an edge in seeking federal funds and expertise for its turnaround efforts. The Promise Zone brings with it a federal liaison to help the designees navigate existing resources and five full time AmeriCorps staff who would be located within City Hall, to help support the Promise Zone initiative.

When People See God Move!

With all the publicity of all of what was going on in Camden, I was contacted by some concern citizens from Trenton, New Jersey who heard that I had a relationship with the Faith-based and Neighborhood Partnerships Department out of the White House and was asked if I could assist them in getting them an audience. I began to spend time in prayer and did my research with the assistance of Minister Angeline Dean. Angeline happened to have had a great deal of knowledge of the cities needs, as well as her relationship with the faith community. I don't believe we would have had such a great response from Trenton's political, community and spiritual leaders if it were not for Minister Dean's involvement.

At the time of my request to the Center for Faith-based Neighborhood and Partnerships Dr. Jannah was on a special assignment, so she graciously connected me with her colleague Mr. Marcus Coleman. He in turn invested a great deal of time in making sure that the key players were put in place. Our first meeting with Mr. Coleman was held at the Mayor's office in Trenton, with standing room only. Some of the people who were in attendance at this meeting, were the acting Mayor at the time George Muschal, Acting Mercer County Prosecutor Angelo Onofri, Dave Leonardis and John Paige from The New Jersey Office of Homeland Security & Preparedness, Wanda Moore, Assistant Attorney General – Director, Office Community Justice at New Jersey Office of the Attorney General, Trenton's Police Director Ralph Rivera Jr., many other political and spiritual leaders which are too many to mention but along with my husband for much needed spiritual support I invited my mentor Rev. Dr. Eve Lynne Fenton and my spiritual father Dr. Abraham Fenton. Following the meeting in the Mayor's office we boarded a bus and was given a tour by the acting Mayor and Community Activist Darren Green who knew the hot spots of the city where criminal activity was prevalent, Darren spends a great deal of time bringing peace in the surrounding communities, his passion for Trenton is like mine for Camden. Success comes when likeminded people work together in unity for the greater good.

The second meeting scheduled for that same day was held that evening at the Grace Cathedral Fellowship Church at 1217 Calhoun Street in Trenton, N.J. Bishop J.D. Brown was our host. Grace Cathedral was such a gracious ministry; we were even assisted with a van to tour the city along with a driver. I was in awe of the support that was afforded us by Bishop Wilcox's the overseer of Grace Cathedral. We possibly had more than one hundred (100) clergy in attendance amongst many others, like representatives from the New Jersey State Police one of whose name was Sergeant First Class Gregory Williams, several others from The New Jersey Office of Homeland Security, and Special Agent Vernon Addison from the Federal Bureau of Investigation (FBI). I had no idea that God was going to use me in this capacity and fill the room with the likes of this crowd.

In April of this year (2015) I partnered with the Mayor of Westampton, NJ Carolyn Chang in obtaining some success for the Burlington County area. I'm presently working with Dr. Jannah and many of her colleagues out of Washington on a recovery plan for Atlantic City, New Jersey. I reached out to her again on behalf of Pastor Eric McCoy and the Fellowship of Churches. With her acceptance and her willingness to look into the concerns of the Clergy we scheduled a forum entitled *"Partnerships and Progress to Help Atlantic City Recover,"* whereas Local, State and Federal Partnerships come together for the Common Good. With major stakeholders at the table we are expecting a great recovery for Atlantic City. Several of the community leaders have agreed to partner with us, for this much needed recovery due to lack of jobs, youth violence and the need for economic community development as well as the prison re-entry problems.

Knocking on the doors of the Federal Government for cities that you don't live in is a bold step of faith, using my blood washed credentials has made it extremely easy.

Have You Been Called?

One thing I know for sure is that when the Lord Jesus Christ tells you to do something and you are willing and obedient it will come to pass. Isaiah 1:19 states, that *"If you are willing and obedient, You shall eat the good of the land."* I stand here today and proclaim that every city that we have assisted has seen the hand of God move bringing the much needed help for recovery. Throughout all of the forums and symposiums that Dr. Jannah who is an ordained minister and I sought to bring some form of relief to, our dependence was definitely the assistance of God through the agency of intense prayer. Intercession was needed in order to go into cities that the enemy had controlled for many years, and he was not going away without an ugly fight.

Many times we reason or do things in our own way, pride, intellect and strength. When we try and see through our own pride and strength we will always fail. Proverbs 16:20 says, *"He who heeds the word wisely will find good, And whoever trusts in the LORD, happy is he."* God continues to use me in ways that in the natural it's hard for me to explain, all I know is that He is no respecter of persons and He searches the earth looking for someone to show Himself strong in those whose heart is perfect toward Him, *"For the eyes of the LORD range throughout the earth to strengthen those whose hearts are fully committed to him."*

Virtue is always manifested through blessings that you have passed on. Nothing will be of any importance to you except what you pass on to others. That is why it is extremely important for you to *"Trust in the LORD with all your heart, and do not lean on your own understanding. In all your ways acknowledge him, and he will make straight your paths. Be not wise in your own eyes; fear the Lord, and turn away from evil"* (Proverbs 3:5-7).

"Wake up and dream! Dream bigger than your imagination can imagine...Then pursue it!"

-JAT

White House Visit to Trenton, New Jersey

Minister Angeline Dean, Bishop J.D. Brown & Me

*"I am the sum total of what I have been
confessing through the years."*

-Joel Osteen

Dave Leornardis with Pastor Jonathan W. Cook
in the Mayor's office in Trenton, New Jersey

Second meeting of the day at Grace Cathedral in Trenton, New Jersey

Atlantic City Recovery Forum
Bishop Robert Hargrove, Dr. Jannah Scott & Me!

"Behold, what manner of love the Father hath bestowed upon us, that we should be called the sons of God therefore the world knoweth us not, because it knew him not. Beloved, now are we the sons of God, and it doth not yet appear what we shall be; but we know that, when he shall appear, we shall be like him; for we shall see him as he is."

(1 John 3:1-2)

CHAPTER 13

The Bride of Christ

The symbolism of marriage is applied to Christ and the body of believers who is known as the church. These are those who have trusted in Jesus Christ as their personal savior and have received eternal life. In the New Testament, Christ, the Bridegroom, has sacrificially and lovingly chosen the church to be His bride. Jesus the Christ desires a relationship with His church both intimately and passionately. We have to refuse all sensual overtones to the Bride of Christ message.

In being an overseer of a woman's ministry I have heard said so often of single women and believe it or not, in my early walk with God as a single, I have said it myself as well. So to help you who have yet to marry single ladies, Jesus is not our lover or boyfriend neither is He our husband. We do not go on "dates" with Jesus. Receiving the "kiss of God's Word" in Song of Solomon Chapter 1 verse 2 has nothing to do with physically kissing God!!! Neither the spiritual interpretation of the Song of Solomon nor references to the "romance of the gospel" have anything to do with sensuality, but with the adventuresome love that is filled with a spirit of abandonment that sacrificially loves and obeys Jesus. An example of this is seen when Paul and Silas sang songs of love to Jesus after being beaten and thrown into prison, *"The crowd joined in attacking them, and the magistrates tore the garments off them and gave orders to beat them with rods. And when they had inflicted many blows upon them, they threw them into prison, ordering the jailer to keep them safely. Having received this order, he put them into the inner prison and fastened their feet in the stocks. About midnight Paul and Silas were praying and singing hymns to God, and the prisoners were listening to them, and suddenly there was a great earthquake, so that the foundations of the prison were shaken. And immediately all the doors were opened, and everyone's bonds were unfastened"* (Acts 16:22-26).

We are not "married' to Jesus in this age. Paul describes believers as betrothed or "engaged" to Jesus. The "consummation" of the marriage is in the age to come when we see Him face to face. Single women do not "marry" Jesus in this age. Even in the age to come, they will not be married to Jesus in a special way that differs from married women or men who love Jesus. There is a great blessing in living single for Jesus, but it is about securing undistracted devotion to Jesus now rather than about "getting married" to Jesus. *"One who is unmarried is concerned about the things of the Lord, how he may please the Lord; but one who is married is concerned about the things of the world, how he may please his wife, and his interests are divided... I say for your own benefit... to promote what is seemly, and to secure undistracted devotion to the Lord"* (1 Cor. 7:32-35, NAS).

John says in Revelation 19:7-8, *"For the wedding of the Lamb has come, and His Bride has made herself ready. Fine linen, bright and clean was given her to wear."* As we live on this earth, those in Christ should be getting ready to become His Bride. Jesus has gone away to prepare a place for us and He will be back, will you be ready? Ephesians 5:22-33 compares the relationship and responsibilities of the husband and wife to the relationship of Jesus and His church. In verse 25 it says for husbands to *"Love your wife as Christ also loved the church,* verse 27 shows the Lord's desire to *"Present to Himself the church in all her glory having no spot or wrinkle or any such thing; but that she would be holy and blameless."* Such an accomplishment would take Jesus' close and personal involvement in our lives, and a passionate response to Him on our part to have such a relationship.

God gives us the opportunity to obey or disobey Him as one way to show our love for Him. *"But of the tree of the knowledge of good and evil you shall not eat, for in the day that you eat of it you shall surely die"* (Gen. 2:17). Eve was deceived by Satan. We are not to be ignorant of Satan's devices or tactics (2 Cor. 2:11). The serpent was more cunning than any beast of the field... he said to the woman, *"Has God indeed said, 'You shall not eat of every tree of the garden'?"...* The serpent said to the woman, *"You will not surely die. For*

God knows that in the day you eat of it your eyes will be opened, and you will be like God, knowing good and evil" (Gen. 3:1-5).

Paul used Eve's deception to show us how Satan leads people astray from pure devotion to Jesus. *"For I betrothed you to one husband, that to Christ I might present you as a pure virgin. But I am afraid, lest as the serpent deceived Eve by his craftiness, your minds should be led astray from the simplicity and purity of devotion to Christ"* (2 Cor. 11:23; NAS). We are beautiful to God in redemption by virtue of who God is and what He is like. God is all loving toward us, and has a great capacity to enjoy His people. Beauty is in the eyes of the beholder. God's personality and perspective is filled with love and generosity. The Bible makes it clear that in the generation in which the Lord returns the Holy Spirit will emphasize Jesus as Bridegroom, King, and Judge. There are many faces to Jesus' personality in ministry, but the Holy Spirit is going to bring into focus Jesus as the Bridegroom God, King and Judge. The challenge will be that there's no contradiction in Jesus as Bridegroom, Jesus as King, and Jesus as Judge. As a bridegroom, He's filled with desire for His people. As King, He manifests His power, and as the Judge, He has zeal to confront everything that hinders love. He will remove everything that gets in the way of love. Because of the gift of righteousness, every believer, when he or she comes to Jesus, stands before God as a chaste virgin. In 2 Corinthians 11:2, Paul tells us that Jesus took away our impurity as a free gift. He gave us His righteousness and He has given us a standing before the Father and before Himself, as a virgin. Pure and chaste here are the same idea. No matter what you did, even if it was as recent as yesterday, by the power of the blood of

Jesus, every born-again believer stands before Him in purity, blameless before Him as His gift. This is true of every sincere believer who is warring against the issues in their lives that are being compromised. They might be stumbling, but they're repenting, confessing, and standing in the righteousness of Jesus. The Scriptures depict an account of ten virgins who were all born again believers. All ten of these believers had lamps. A lamp speaks of the ability to bring light to others, ultimately highlighting the importance of ministry. In other words, all ten of these believers have functioning ministries with light-bearing ministries bringing light to others in a time of darkness. They're born-again believers who were called to the ministry by virtue of their born again experience. It teaches us to say no to ungodliness and worldly passions, and to live self-controlled, upright and godly lives in this present age. While patiently waiting, for the glorious appearing of our great Savior, Jesus Christ, who gave himself for us to redeem us from all wickedness. To purify for Himself a people that are His very own, eagerly to do what is good.

It's in the Bible that He's the Bridegroom God. Your relationship with Jesus needs to be the primary desire of your heart—not your ministry, or anything else. Jesus mentioned the bridal relationship three times, but always from the perspective of the Bridegroom (Mt. 9:15; 22:2; 25:1). Jesus and John the Baptist spoke of the Bridegroom rather than the Bride. By seeing Jesus as our Bridegroom God, He is then able to awaken our understanding of who we are before Him as His cherished Bride. We see the truth of our identity by understanding His. *"Beholding... the glory of the Lord, [we] are being transformed"* (2 Cor. 3:18).

In order to experience the transformation there has to be sacrifice, you'll have to pass up what may appear to be opportunities. It means taking time to grow in understanding His desire for you as a Bridegroom God. I found out that over time I had to miss certain opportunities for growth, certain social opportunities; there even were some relational as well as financial opportunities. Why? Even though God promises you that, it's still a promise about your assignment. Your number one desire has to be you and Him: Him touching you, you feeling His love, and you returning it back with all your heart. There's nothing more powerful in the world than to feel the love of God and have the ability to love Him with all of your heart. That's the most powerful way to live. It' time to fall ***"In Love Under New Management!"***

My Wedding Day!

In Loving Memory
Of My Nephew
Robert Lee Greene, Jr.
October 22, 1989 – January 15, 2015

In Loving Memory
Of My Sister
Joy M. Delmage
November 4, 1952 – February 15, 2015

Praise for "In Love Under New Management."

Pastor Gwendolyn Ann Cook presents to the body of Christ a book based on her vast experience, which includes seasons of suffering and persecution she has had to endure. In a day of complacency and compromise *Love under new management* is a breath of fresh air to the body of Christ.

Dr. Robert Fulton Hargrove, II
Senior Pastor of
Grace Family Church
Atlantic City, New Jersey

Love under new management is a book that will transform your thinking about true and authentic love. In reading this book, Pastor Cook influences you to increase your spirituality, and in this season of your life, catapult you to the dimension, that God has ordained for you. As I began to walk through the pages of this "Literary Masterpiece," it was difficult not embrace the information as I step by step traveled through it. From assessing your life through "Unconditional Surrender" and dealing with the negatives that imposes on one's spiritual growth and maturity in God to becoming an able vessel in the word, to personify and bring to life the Scriptures in "The Bride of Christ," where it says in 1 John 3: 2-3, "We Shall See Him As He Is" in us. The pure love of Jesus Christ will cause you to mirror yourself in his Word until, the two hearts become one, and at that juncture in your Christian journey, you'll find yourself ultimately living your best life through Christ's Love, Under New Management.

Lynn Davis,
Senior Pastor of
Harvest Church, Inc.
Blackwood, New Jersey
Founder/Executive Director of the
Grace I. Ross-Lewis Resource Center

About the Book

As you read "In Love Under New Management" you will meet a woman who dares to live out her divine purpose. After enduring sixteen years with an issue of blood and a number of other medical issues, she was led to depend on her faith, which ultimately caused her to obtain her healing. Through her own transparency Gwen will also help you discover that you're beginning does not necessarily determine your end. Gwen grew up in a loving military family, being the youngest of five siblings of four girls and one boy. During her adolescence years she suffered with an extremely low self-image of herself while struggling with her weight. After several years of dieting with no success she redirected her focus on how she could assist others to live out their God given assignment and in giving of herself to others she was able to witness some of her own successes. From the beginning to the end, "In Love Under New Management" will keep you on the edge of your seat.

Printed in the United States
By Bookmasters